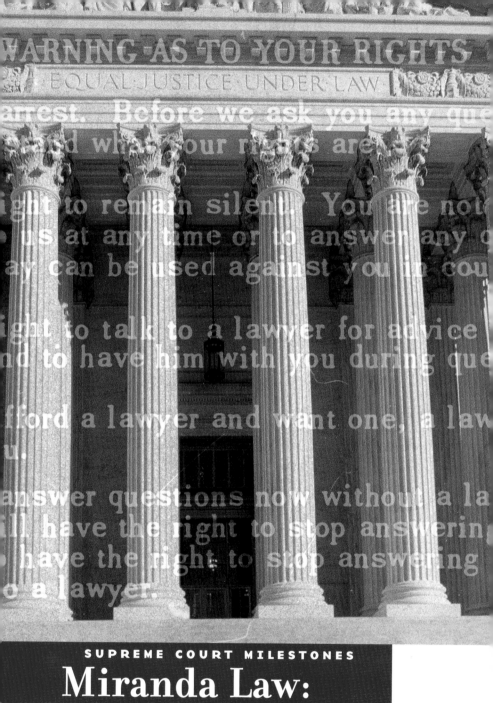

WARNING AS TO YOUR RIGHTS

EQUAL JUSTICE UNDER LAW

arrest.   Before we ask you any que
nd what your rights are

ight to remain silent.   You are not
us at any time or to answer any o
ay can be used against you in cou

ight to talk to a lawyer for advice
nd to have him with you during que

fford a lawyer and want one, a law
u.

answer questions now without a la
ill have the right to stop answering
have the right to stop answering
e a lawyer.

SUPREME COURT MILESTONES

Miranda Law:
THE RIGHT TO REMAIN SILENT

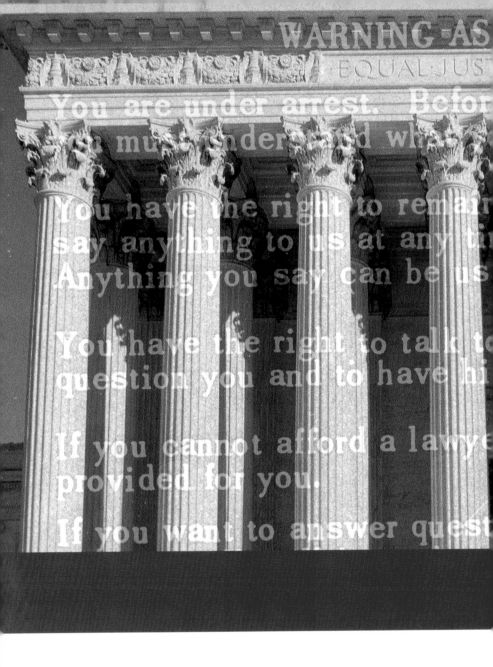

SUPREME COURT MILESTONES

Miranda Law:

THE RIGHT TO REMAIN SILENT

RON FRIDELL

Marshall Cavendish
Benchmark
New York

With special thanks to Professor David M. O'Brien of the Woodrow Wilson Department of Politics at the University of Virginia for reviewing the text of this book.

Marshall Cavendish Benchmark
99 White Plains Road
Tarrytown, NY 10591
www.marshallcavendish.us

Library of Congress Cataloging-in-Publication Data • Fridell, Ron. • Miranda law : the right to remain silent / by Ron Fridell.—1st ed. • p. cm.—(Supreme Court milestones) • Summary: "Describes the historical context of the Miranda versus Arizona Supreme Court case, detailing the claims made by both sides as well as the outcome, and including excerpts from the Supreme Court justices' decisions and relevant sidebars"—Provided by publisher. • Includes bibliographical references and index. • ISBN 0-7614-1942-X • 1. Miranda, Ernesto—Trials, litigation, etc.—Juvenile literature. 2. Right to counsel—United States--Juvenile literature. 3. Confession (Law)—United States--Juvenile literature. 4. Police questioning—United States—Juvenile literature. I. Title. II. Series. • KF224.M54F75 2005 • 345.73'056—dc22 • 2005001156

Photo research by Candlepants, Inc.

The photographs in this book are used by permission and through the courtesy of: *AP/Wide World Photos*: 6, 83, 121; *Bridgeman Art Library/Private Collection, Ken Walsh*; 19; *The Image Works/Topham*: 20; *Getty Images*: Hulton Archive, 22; MPI, 36, 92; New York Times Co./George Tames; 54; *Corbis*: Stapleton Collection, 23; Bettman, 35, 42, 43, 44, 47, 51, 73, 75, 76, 88, 90; Bob Daemmerich, 106; *Sy Snarr Photography*: 109.

Series design by Sonia Chaghatzbanian
Printed in China • 135642

contents

one   The *Miranda* Rule   7

TWO   You Have the Right to Remain Silent   18

THree   You Have the Right to Counsel   33

four   Filing the Case   55

FIVe   The Oral Arguments   64

SIX   The Ruling   77

seven   Reactions to the Ruling   91

eIGHT   Exceptions and Extensions   97

nine   *Miranda* Is Challenged   107

Ten   *Miranda* Today   113

Notes   129

Further Information   135

Bibliography   137

Index   139

ERNESTO MIRANDA WAS A SMALL-TIME CRIMINAL WHOSE NAME WILL LONG OUTLIVE HIS DEEDS BECAUSE OF THE FAMOUS SUPREME COURT CASE.

one
THE *MIRANDA* RULE

ERNESTO ARTHUR MIRANDA lived the life of a classic career criminal. It was brief and brutal, and he spent much of it shut away from society.

During his life of crime he did nothing to set himself apart from the ordinary violent criminal. It was fate that turned him into the key figure in a landmark U.S. Supreme Court case.

Fate also turned Miranda's name into a three-syllable word repeated thousands of times in newspaper headlines and television shows, as in "Did you read them their *Miranda* rights?" It even got turned into a verb: "Yes, the suspects have been Mirandized." Miranda himself became so famous that people paid him for his autograph.

When you make a timeline of the events in Miranda's life, they look like stepping-stones on his own personal road to ruin. He was born and raised in Phoenix, Arizona. He was fourteen when he got nabbed for his first serious crime. That was in 1954. He'd just graduated from eighth grade when he was caught stealing a car in Phoenix.

Auto theft is a felony, a crime punishable by a year or more in jail. But this was Miranda's first felony conviction, so the judge sentenced him to a period of probation instead. During this time Miranda would remain free only as long as he behaved himself.

It wasn't long before Miranda got himself into more trouble. The crime was another felony—burglary, and this time the judge had Miranda put away. Since he was under eighteen, he did his first stretch at a juvenile detention facility, the Arizona State Industrial School for Boys.

As soon as Miranda was released, he took up where he'd left off. Between 1956 and 1961 he was convicted of crimes in five different states. His offenses were more serious now—and violent. Among them were assault and rape. During these years Miranda kept moving in and out of prison, rarely holding down a job for more than a few weeks.

Then, in August 1962, his life appeared to take a turn for the better. Miranda got his first steady job, driving a truck for a fruit and vegetable company. He also settled down with a woman named Twila Hoffman, becoming her common-law husband and her daughter's stepfather. And together, Miranda and Hoffman had a child of their own.

Things were nowhere near as normal as they appeared, though. Miranda was leading a secret criminal life. At night he cruised the streets of Phoenix looking for women. Among his crimes against women were kidnapping, robbery, and rape.

THE CRIMES

Two of these crimes would help make him infamous. The first was an armed robbery. At 8:30 PM on November 27, 1962, he robbed a young woman of eight dollars at knifepoint.

Then on March 3, 1963, he committed the second, more serious crime. Late at night, an eighteen-year-old woman finished working behind the refreshment counter of the Paramount Theater and stepped onto a Phoenix city bus, headed for home. Shortly after she stepped off, a 1953

Packard sedan pulled up and a man scrambled out and forced her into the back seat, where he bound her hand and foot. Then he drove her out of Phoenix and into the desert to rape her. The man was Ernesto Miranda.

Ten days later, police arrested Miranda for robbery and rape. They handcuffed him and drove him to a police station, where they put him into a four-person lineup, at the extreme left. The young woman he had raped looked the four men over. She could see them clearly but they could not see her. She said that the man on the extreme left resembled her attacker, but she could not be positive.

The confession

The suspect was taken to Interrogation Room No. 2 of the detective bureau. The two officers who arrested him sat him down, and Miranda asked about the lineup. What happened? The officers lied to him. They said his victim had positively identified him as her assailant.

At this point we should note that the arresting officers, Carroll Cooley and Wilfred Young, had not informed the suspect of two of his constitutional rights: his right to remain silent and his right to speak with an attorney. Three years later, the U.S. Supreme Court would make these two constitutional rights the foundation of the *Miranda* rule.

Then the young woman was brought into the interrogation room to face Miranda for the first time. As they looked at each other, the officers asked Miranda if this was the girl he had raped. Later, Miranda would claim that he answered "Yes" only because he had been told that she already had identified him.

The moment she heard Miranda's voice, the young woman knew that he was the one. Now she truly had made a positive identification. After a short interrogation,

THE EXCLUSIONARY RULE

Defense attorneys who ask judges to suppress evidence against their clients are relying on the exclusionary rule. This rule is based on a series of U.S. Supreme Court rulings that all make the same point: Any evidence obtained illegally cannot be used in a court of law—and that includes coerced confessions. This rule, which is unique to the U.S. criminal justice system, has been a continuing source of controversy. Some people blame it for favoring the rights of criminals over the rights of victims. Others say that without the exclusionary rule, the rights of all citizens would be put at risk.

Miranda confessed to the rape and to the knifepoint robbery as well. The officers typed out Miranda's confession to both crimes word for word and gave it to him to sign. At the top of the first page were these words:

> "I, _____, do hereby swear that I make this statement voluntarily and of my own free will, with no threats, coercion, or promises of immunity, and with full knowledge of my legal rights, understanding any statement I make may be used against me."

THE Pre-Trial Hearing

Miranda's trial was scheduled for June 1963. Since he could not afford to pay a lawyer, the court appointed one for him, free of charge. The state of Arizona would pay Alvin Moore a fee of one hundred dollars to defend Miranda. Moore was not happy with the state's meager fee or with his client's low moral character and long criminal record.

Still, Moore did his sworn duty as a defense lawyer: to give his client, no matter who he might be, the best defense possible. First, Moore objected to the confession. He said it should be suppressed—excluded from evidence in the jury trial. Why? Because the confession was coerced, Moore claimed. It had been produced by intimidation, threats, and pressure; a confession could be used as evidence in court only if it was made voluntarily, without coercion. Furthermore, said Moore, the officers never informed Miranda of his constitutional rights.

Moore's objection was handled in a pre-trial hearing in front of the judge. As the name suggests, a pre-trial hearing occurs before the actual trial, and its purpose is to address any issues that need to be settled before the trial.

In this case the issue was Miranda's confession. If the judge accepted Moore's motion, the confession would not be used as evidence. The jury would never hear anything about it.

Moore gave the judge his side of the argument, explaining why the confession was coerced and should be excluded from evidence. Then the prosecuting attorney gave his side. Miranda had signed a paper stating that he was aware of his legal rights, the prosecuting attorney said. That meant the confession was voluntary and should be included as evidence.

After hearing the arguments, the judge dismissed Moore's objection. Miranda's confession was voluntary, he ruled, and the prosecution could present it to the jury.

THE jury trial

Miranda's jury trial for armed robbery and rape began on June 20, 1963. During the trial, Moore cross-examined officers Cooley and Young. He aggressively questioned them about the damaging testimony they had given in regard to his client.

No, they admitted, they had not advised Miranda of his constitutional rights to remain silent and to talk with a lawyer.

Moore wanted to know why not.

Miranda was an ex-convict, the officers answered, so he already knew about his rights. He already knew he didn't have to answer their questions.

Moore asked if they had made any threats or promises to Miranda in exchange for a confession.

Absolutely not, the officers replied. They never tried to trick or coerce the suspect in any way. All they did was ask simple, straightforward questions until he confessed. And not once did he ask to speak to a lawyer.

Just before the members of a jury leave the courtroom to confer and reach a verdict, the trial judge gives them instructions. The judge in Miranda's trial made sure the jury understood that they were to treat Ernesto Miranda's confession as valid evidence. Just because the police had not advised Miranda of his rights, the judge insisted, that did not make the confession involuntary. With this instruction in mind, the jury found Miranda guilty as charged, and the judge sentenced him to from twenty to thirty years in prison.

Shortly thereafter, Ernesto Miranda became inmate number 27555 at the Arizona State Prison at Florence, sixty miles southeast of Phoenix. Ernesto Miranda was about to begin a long legal battle, as he worked his way through the appeals court system from bottom to top—and also worked his way into history.

THE APPEALS PROCESS

The trial court that convicted Ernesto Miranda sits on the bottom rung of the federal criminal justice system ladder. Perched at the very top is the U.S. Supreme Court.

In between are several appeals courts, also known as appellate courts. Each state has its own appeals court system, with a state supreme court and one or more appeals courts below it. Alongside these state appeals courts are federal appeals courts. These federal appeals courts may review state cases that have passed through the state appeals courts, provided a federal constitutional issue has been raised.

Appeals courts have a different purpose than trial courts. They do not decide a defendant's guilt or innocence. Instead, a panel of judges reviews the original trial in order to rule on whether the decision was fair. Appeals courts may also review lower appeals court rulings. The judges ask: Were all parties treated fairly? Did they act within the law? Were someone's constitutional rights violated, and if so, were these violations serious enough to warrant reversing the trial court verdict?

The side that loses a criminal case may appeal the decision. The *Miranda* appeals cases were called *Miranda* v. *Arizona* because Miranda was the loser. He appealed the guilty verdict that put him in prison. (If Miranda had won his case in the lower court, then the state could have appealed. In that event the appeals case would have been called *Arizona* v. *Miranda*.)

When Miranda lost, his lawyer filed the appeals petition to have the guilty verdict reversed. This made Miranda the petitioner. The state of Arizona was the respondent, the side responding to the appeal. The state's attorney asked that the trial court's guilty verdict remain in place.

Miranda's appeals did not go well. The Arizona State Supreme Court ruled that the trial court had been fair. Officers Cooley and Young had not coerced Miranda's confession. This left Miranda with two choices: Give up and do his twenty-to-thirty year stretch, or appeal to the highest court in the land.

THE U.S. SUPreme COURT RULING

Miranda v. *Arizona* was argued before the U.S. Supreme Court and decided in 1966. After reviewing the rulings by the trial court and appeals courts, the U.S. Supreme Court sided with Miranda. The trial court's guilty verdict was reversed, and the case was sent back to the state of Arizona for retrial.

Not only did Miranda himself win, but his personal victory amounted to a victory for criminal suspects in general. The Miranda ruling was all about controlling police power and protecting criminal suspects. The Court's

U.S. supreme court profile

The Supreme Court is the highest court in the United States. Among its defining characteristics are the following:

- The Supreme Court is created by Article III, Sections 1 and 2, of the U.S. Constitution.
- The Court meets regularly in the Supreme Court Building in Washington, D.C.
- It has nine members, known as justices. One is the chief justice, and the other eight are associate justices. The justices are appointed for life by the president, with the advice and consent of the Senate.
- The Supreme Court is charged with ensuring that all citizens receive equal justice under the law and that the rights guaranteed them by the Constitution are protected.
- Juries are not involved in Supreme Court cases. Instead, the Court reviews lower court decisions that raise conflicts between the Constitution and federal or state law. Its rulings are meant to preserve the Constitution.
- Once the Court makes a ruling, the other U.S. courts are expected to follow its decisions in similar cases.

Miranda v. *Arizona* ruling was tens of thousands of words long. Here is the most important part:

> The person in custody must, prior to interrogation, be clearly informed that he has the right to remain silent, and that anything he says will be used against him in court; he must be clearly informed that he has the right to consult with a lawyer and to have the lawyer with him during interrogation, and that, if he is indigent [poor], a lawyer will be appointed to represent him.

These words formed the basis of the now famous *Miranda* rule, designed to prevent police officers from coercing confessions. "Unless adequate preventive measures are taken to dispel the compulsion inherent in custodial surroundings," the Court warned, "no statement obtained from the defendant can truly be the product of his free choice."

After *Miranda*, police officers would have to be sure that suspects understood their rights. Otherwise, the officers ran the risk of having the suspect's confession excluded from evidence at the trial.

The *Miranda* rule remains in force today. Anyone who watches television cop shows has seen police officers read these rights to suspects. Law enforcement agencies at all levels—local, state, and federal—have accepted the *Miranda* rule as a standard part of their everyday work.

But this is not the whole story. The story behind the *Miranda* rule begins hundreds of years ago in another country when kings and queens made the laws and had them enforced. It is a colorful story with a host of criminals and victims. It also features law enforcement officers, attorneys, judges and justices, reporters, professors, and political leaders, who all wrestle with the rights and responsibilities of constitutional law. This book tells their story.

TWO
YOU HAVE THE RIGHT TO
REMAIN SILENT

Miranda v. *Arizona* (1966) was a landmark U.S. Supreme Court ruling. In other words, it set precedent—it influenced rulings in a great many cases that followed. Deciding *Miranda* was a tough and tricky task. The nine U.S. Supreme Court justices who helped shape the *Miranda* ruling had to balance two conflicting concerns. The first was protecting the public from criminals. The second was protecting criminal suspects from abuses by law enforcement officers and trial courts.

Miranda was also a carefully documented decision. The justices who made the 1966 ruling reached well back into history for help. Their ruling was based on what they called "principles long recognized and applied in other settings." In other words, their ruling was grounded in rulings from past cases. Some of these cases dealt with the Fifth Amendment right to remain silent: "No person shall be . . . compelled in any criminal case to be a witness against himself."

These cases included the *Lilburn* Star Chamber case (1637), *Brown* v. *Walker* (1896), *Brown* v. *Mississippi* (1936), and *Malloy* v. *Hogan* (1964). The *Miranda* justices cited, or referred to, each of these cases in their ruling.

Miranda and the Star Chamber

The first case looked at was England's notorious Court of the Star Chamber. Today, England's royal family cannot charge, arrest, and punish people. But it could in the seventeenth century. The Court of the Star Chamber was an arm of the ruling monarchy that operated on its own, outside of normal British law. It specialized in trying and punishing people who would not obey the royal family's wishes. Confessions were often coerced and sentences could be harsh and brutal.

England's seventeenth century Court of the Star Chamber was notorious for doling out harsh sentences for minor crimes, often based on coerced confessions.

The names of the Iury
of life and death.

JOHN LILBURN (C. 1614-1657), A PURITAN ACTIVIST AND PAMPHLETEER, WAS
SENTENCED TO BE WHIPPED AND THEN STOOD IN PILLORY UNTIL HE CON-
FESSED HIS CRIME. LILBURN SAID HE WAS NOT GUILTY, BUT THE BISHOPS
WERE GUILTY OF CRUELTY.

The *Miranda* ruling cited one Star Chamber case in particular. In 1637, publisher John Lilburn was accused of selling books that challenged the monarchy's authority. The monarchy struck back by sending Lilburn to the Star Chamber. His accusers insisted that he confess. When Lilburn refused, they threatened him with torture, but Lilburn still refused. "[N]o man's conscience ought to be racked by oaths imposed, to answer to questions concerning himself in matters criminal, or pretended to be so," he said. Lilburn would not cooperate. He would not become a witness against himself.

Lilburn was then whipped, fined, and imprisoned. But while he was incarcerated, British public opinion turned against the Star Chamber, and the monarchy backed down. After serving four years in prison, Lilburn was released, and the Court of the Star Chamber was abolished. After that, only voluntary confessions could be used as evidence in trials. No one could be coerced into incriminating himself. While this principle against self-incrimination was never actually written down, it became a part of English common law. Common laws are principles of law based on tradition. Even though they are not written down, courts still follow them.

Miranda and the Fifth Amendment

The *Miranda* ruling cited the British *Lilburn* case as an example of a government denying a citizen the right to be protected against self-incrimination. The ruling went on to tell how the English colonists who came to North America in the 1600s brought the common law principle of protection from self-incrimination along with them. Later, the colonists' descendants went a step further. By including it in the Fifth Amendment of the Bill of Rights, they made it a written, constitutional law.

THE CHAMBER OF TORTURE

England's Court of the Star Chamber was infamous for handing out severe punishments for minor offenses. A London merchant was heavily fined and imprisoned for six years for simply criticizing the nation's taxation policies out loud. All he said was that merchants are "in no part of the world so screwed and wrung [by high taxes] as in England."

Some punishments were strangely cruel. The Court of the Star Chamber threw a man who objected to eating pork on religious grounds into prison, where he was fed nothing but the flesh of pigs.

THE RACK.

CUTHBERT SIMPSON SUFFERS ON THE RACK IN THE TOWER OF LONDON DURING THE MARIAN PERSECUTION, 1558. HE WAS BURNED AT SMITHFIELD, ENGLAND, IN THE SAME YEAR.

A number of the Star Chamber's prisoners ended up on the rack, a wooden frame to which the prisoner's limbs were lashed with cords. This frame was then slowly stretched, and the prisoner's bound body along with it, until the joints of the wrists and ankles were pulled apart. Other prisoners had a thick rope full of knots tied around their head and twisted. The object of these excruciating tortures was to get stubborn prisoners to confess to the crime they'd been charged with.

THIS WOODCUT PRINTING OF A VICTIM UNDERGOING ESTRAPADE TORTURE SHOWS HOW SUSPECTED CRIMINALS WERE DEALT WITH LONG BEFORE THE NOTION EXISTED THAT THOSE ARRESTED HAD ANY RIGHTS.

Torturers also cut off suspects' body parts. In 1632, lawyer William Prynne was stripped of his university degrees and his license to practice law. Then his ears were cut off, and he was imprisoned for life without books, pen, ink, or paper. His offense? He had criticized the monarchy.

As *Brown* v. *State of Mississippi* (1936), stated, "The Constitution recognized the evils that lay behind these practices and prohibited them in this country."

Looking back to Lilburn and the Star Chamber, the *Miranda* ruling explained the principle against self-incrimination: "[O]ur accusatory system of criminal justice demands that the government seeking to punish an individual produce the evidence against him by its own independent labors, rather than by the cruel, simple expedient of compelling it from his own mouth."

coerced confessions

The justices' concerns with coerced confessions come from a very real concern: the chance that police will abuse their power. To detect and apprehend criminals, law enforcement officers must have legal powers that ordinary citizens cannot have. These include the power to arrest criminal suspects and question them about the crimes they may have committed, hoping to get them to confess.

A lawful confession is a powerful piece of evidence. In the U.S. criminal justice system, the defendant does not have to prove his innocence. The burden of proof rests entirely with the authorities. They must prove the defendant guilty beyond a reasonable doubt, and a signed confession gives them precious proof in the suspect's own words. A confession makes the prosecution's job much easier. Even with no other evidence to present to the judge and jury, prosecutors can get a conviction with a believable confession, despite a suspect's subsequent plea of "not guilty" in court.

This presents the police with a strong temptation to violate a suspect's Fifth Amendment right against self-incrimination. Most police officers operate within the law, but police officers are human. Convinced of a suspect's guilt, some of them sometimes give in to temptation and turn to coercion to force a precious confession.

THE FIFTH AMENDMENT

The Fifth Amendment states:

No person shall be held to answer for a capital, or otherwise infamous crime, unless on a presentment or indictment of a grand jury, except in cases arising in the land or naval forces, or in the militia, when in actual service in time of war or public danger; nor shall any person be subject for the same offense to be twice put in jeopardy of life or limb; nor shall be compelled in any criminal case to be a witness against himself, nor be deprived of life, liberty, or property, without due process of law; nor shall private property be taken for public use, without just compensation.easier.

Brown v. *Walker*, a U.S. Supreme Court ruling from 1896, speaks of ". . . the temptation to press the witness unduly, to browbeat him if he be timid or reluctant, to push him into a corner, and to entrap him into fatal contradictions." Together, these forceful tactics mentioned in *Brown* are known as "the third degree."

THE THIRD DEGREE

A 1931 U.S. government document, "The Report on Lawlessness in Law Enforcement," stated that the third degree was widespread among U.S. law enforcement officers at the time. The report came from the Wickersham Commission, which President Herbert Hoover had assigned to investigate law enforcement problems. It was part of a larger document known as the Wickersham Report.

The report documented events of police using physical and psychological coercion to force confessions. In some cities suspects were routinely beaten, threatened with lynching, and locked away in rat-infested cells. This was especially true where African-American suspects were concerned, the report stated.

The 1966 *Miranda* ruling cited *Brown* v. *Walker* and the Wickersham Report. To show that these third-degree tactics were still in use, the ruling cited a recent (1966) example: "Only recently in Kings County, New York, the police brutally beat, kicked and placed lighted cigarette butts on the back of a potential witness under interrogation for the purpose of securing a statement incriminating a third party."

Police brutality also threatens the quality of police work. The Wickersham Report quoted law enforcement officials as saying, "It is a short cut and makes the police lazy and unenterprising," and "If you use your fists, you are not so likely to use your wits."

A Lawless Era

The 1930s was a particularly lawless era in American history. One reason for this was the Eighteenth Amendment to the Constitution, which took effect in 1920. This Amendment prohibited the manufacture and sale of beer, wine, and other alcoholic beverages in the nation.

The Eighteenth Amendment was repealed (taken back) in 1933. In the meantime, prohibition led to gangs of well-organized, armed criminals manufacturing and delivering thousands of gallons of liquor illegally each day. These gangs would battle over territory, killing each other in the process. Prohibition placed added pressure on law enforcement authorities to put violent criminals behind bars.

The report concluded by stating, "The third degree brutalizes the police, hardens the prisoner against society, and lowers the esteem in which the administration of justice is held by the public." The *Miranda* ruling agreed, quoting again from the Wickersham Report: "Not only does the use of the third degree involve a flagrant violation of law by the officers of the law, but it involves also the dangers of false confessions."

The 1931 Wickersham Report dealt only with cases in state courts. Defendants in federal trials were already protected from coerced confessions by the Fifth Amendment. But in 1931, defendants in state trials could not count on these protections. Each state had its own bill of rights, and each state was free to enforce those rights as it saw fit. Even if a state violated a defendant's Fifth Amendment rights, the U.S. Supreme Court would not interfere. It maintained a strictly hands-off attitude.

The 1931 Wickersham Report helped change this attitude. Shortly after the report was issued, the U.S. Supreme Court began accepting appeals that focused on what made confessions used in state trials voluntary and not coerced.

Brown V. *MISSISSIPPI* (1936)

This change in attitude helped save defendants from false imprisonment at the state level. Among the saved were three poor, illiterate African-American men indicted for murder in the state of Mississippi. One, named Arthur Ellington, was hung from a tree and whipped until he confessed. The others, Ed Brown and Henry Shields, were taken to jail, forced to strip naked, and then beaten until they, too, confessed. At trial all three were found guilty and sentenced to death. They appealed to the Mississippi Supreme Court, but that court upheld their convictions.

False confessions

In past history, false confessions were a common occurrence. In seventeenth century England, prisoners were forced to plead guilty by torture if necessary in the notorious Court of the Star Chamber. In the Massachusetts colony in 1692, people accused of witchcraft were also tortured to confess.

Today, false confessions are relatively rare, but they do occur. Some can be explained by a suspect's age. Juveniles may be easily intimidated because of their youth and lack of experience. Their interrogators may lead them to believe that by confessing, they can simply go home and put their problems behind them.

False confessions also come from people with mental disabilities, who often are dependent upon figures of authority. They may be manipulated into false confessions because of their eagerness to please. In 1979, Jerry Frank Townsend, a twenty-seven-year-old man who suffered from mental retardation, confessed to six murders. Years later, new evidence turned up exonerating Frank, and he was released from a Florida prison in 2001, after serving twenty-two years for crimes he did not commit.

Adults of normal mental ability also can be made to confess to crimes they did not commit. After long periods of harsh interrogation, they may give in to exhaustion and falsely confess simply to bring an end to their ordeal.

But the U.S. Supreme Court reversed their convictions. "The rack and torture chamber may not be substituted for the witness stand," the Court ruled. "It would be difficult to conceive of methods more revolting to the sense of justice than those taken to procure the confessions of these petitioners, and the use of the confessions . . . was a clear denial of due process [of law]."

Brown v. *Mississippi* marked the first time the Court reversed a conviction in a state criminal trial because of a coerced confession. It would not be the last. Defendants in state courts could now expect some of the same rights of due process as those in federal courts.

MALLOY V. HOGAN (1964)

The *Miranda* justices cited *Brown* in their ruling. They also cited *Malloy* v. *Hogan*. The petitioner, William Malloy, was ordered to testify before a government official in the Superior Court of Hartford County, Connecticut. The official was investigating illegal gambling activities. Since Malloy was already on probation for a gambling conviction, he was in a sticky spot. Malloy feared that if he told authorities what he knew about these illegal activities, he would get himself in trouble. He might end up testifying against himself. So he refused to answer the official's questions on the Fifth Amendment grounds that his answers might incriminate him.

Malloy was found in contempt of court and sent to prison until he agreed to change his mind and testify. The imprisoned Malloy appealed to the U.S. Supreme Court, and in 1964 it set him free. The Court's reasons were similar to those used in *Brown* v. *Mississippi* some thirty years earlier. The Fourteenth Amendment "due process" clause meant that the state could not deny Malloy his Fifth

due process of law

The term "due process of law" comes from the Fifth Amendment to the Constitution, ratified in 1791, and the Fourteenth Amendment, ratified in 1868. The Fifth Amendment states that no person shall be punished for a crime without first being officially charged and fairly tried in a court of law. It prohibits the federal government, in any criminal case, from depriving any person "of life, liberty, or property, without due process of law." The Fourteenth Amendment extends this prohibition to state governments. Due process is often referred to as the guarantee that each person shall have his or her "day in court."

Amendment right against self-incrimination. Malloy had the constitutional right to remain silent.

The *Miranda* justices used all these cases and the Wickersham Report to help lay the Fifth Amendment, right-to-remain-silent foundation for their landmark 1966 ruling. But that's only half the foundation. The *Miranda* ruling is built on another basic constitutional right.

THREE
YOU HAVE THE RIGHT TO COUNSEL

THE *Miranda* JUSTICES ALSO BUILT a Sixth Amendment foundation of cases for their 1966 ruling. These cases included *Powell* v. *Alabama* (1932), *Betts* v. *Brady* (1942), *Gideon* v. *Wainwright* (1963), and *Escobedo* v. *Illinois* (1964). Let's look at them now.

The Sixth Amendment guarantees the right to an attorney in a criminal trial: "In all criminal prosecutions, the accused shall enjoy the right . . . to have the Assistance of Counsel [a lawyer] for his defence."

This Sixth Amendment right to counsel has a special purpose. It is meant to help equalize the unequal contest between the defendant and the State. Think about this: Ernesto Miranda, a solitary individual, versus Arizona, the vast legal machinery of an entire state. Criminal lawyers' offices are lined with row upon row of law books. How could a defendant in a criminal case possibly understand those thousands upon thousands of pages of legal rules and regulations well enough to successfully defend himself in a court of law?

In all federal courts, criminal defendants were already protected by the Sixth Amendment before the *Miranda* case. If they could not afford to hire a lawyer, the federal government would appoint one for them.

But they were not protected in all state courts. Each

state was free to interpret the Sixth Amendment in its own way. Some states chose to deny poor defendants the right to an attorney, even in capital cases, where the punishment could be death.

THE SCOTTSBOrO BOYS

One of these states was Alabama. As we know, the U.S. Supreme Court was reluctant to reverse rulings made by state courts until the 1930s. Then the Court's attitude began to change.

The change in regard to the right to counsel began with the Court's 1932 *Powell* v. *Alabama* ruling. The defendants were African American, as they were in *Brown* v. *Mississippi*. This time there were nine defendants, all young, poor, and illiterate.

Events in the *Powell* case unfolded this way. The Southern Railroad's Chattanooga freight train was heading through Alabama for Memphis, Tennessee. The year was 1931 and the United States was in the crippling grip of the Great Depression. Poor people were desperately looking for work, and freight trains provided free illegal transportation, provided you didn't get caught.

Among the freight train's passengers that day were a number of young people traveling to different cities in search of jobs. Some were white; some were black. Whether by accident or on purpose, a white man stepped on a black man's hand, and a racial brawl erupted.

The black men threw most of the white men from the train. The angry whites made their way to the nearest town and reported the incident to authorities, who phoned ahead. An armed posse awaited the train as it pulled into the Paint Rock, Alabama, station. When two white women on the train said they had been raped by a gang of twelve

In 1931, nine young black men were falsely accused—and convicted—of raping two young women on a train heading through Alabama to Memphis. They became nationally known as the Scottsboro Boys, a name that came from the Alabama town in which they were jailed.

black men armed with knives and pistols, all the black men on the train were rounded up. The next day's newspaper headline read:

ALL NEGROES POSITIVELY IDENTIFIED BY GIRLS AND ONE WHITE BOY WHO WAS HELD PRISONER WITH PISTOL AND KNIVES WHILE NINE BLACK FIENDS COMMITTED REVOLTING CRIME

The headline's extreme language gives us an idea of what race relations were like in the southern United States

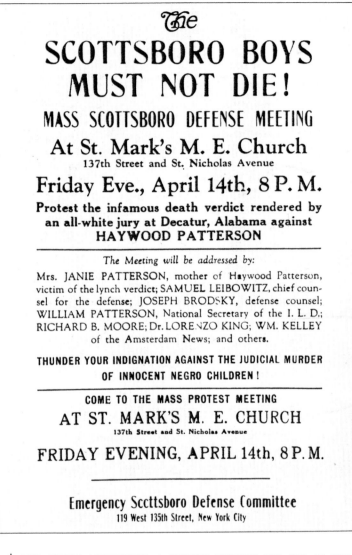

A 1931 POSTER ADVERTISING A DEFENSE MEETING FOR ONE OF THE SCOTTSBORO BOYS. THEY WERE A GROUP OF AFRICAN-AMERICAN TEENS FALSELY ACCUSED OF RAPING TWO WHITE GIRLS IN ALABAMA.

at the time. The case attracted national attention, and the nine defendants became known as the Scottsboro Boys. The name came from the Alabama town where they were jailed. The state tried them in groups of two and three. Meanwhile, a white mob estimated at ten thousand gathered round the courthouse.

The two attorneys appointed for the nine poor defendants made poor criminal defense lawyers. Stephen Roddy's specialty was real estate, and Milo Moody, known for his forgetfulness, had not tried a court case in decades.

Still, the nine defendants looked as if they might be found innocent after all. The only evidence against them came from the two girls' testimony. But the doctor who examined them, two hours after the alleged assaults took place, found no signs that they had been beaten and bloodied, as they claimed.

Each of the three trials was completed in a day's time. Eight of the Scottsboro Boys were found guilty and sentenced to death. Only Roy Wright, age twelve, was let go. A year later, the Alabama Supreme Court agreed with all but one of the eight convictions.

POWELL V. ALABAMA (1932)

This left seven of the original nine Scottsboro Boys still behind bars. Their convictions were appealed to the U.S. Supreme Court under the name *Powell* v. *Alabama*. Powell stood for one of the Scottsboro boys, Ozie Powell. In 1932 the Court found in their favor, reversing their convictions. The most important part of the Court's ruling lies in these words:

> [I]n a capital case, where the defendant is unable to employ counsel, and is incapable adequately of making his own defense because of ignorance,

feeble-mindedness, illiteracy, or the like, it is the duty of the court, whether requested or not, to assign counsel for him as a necessary requisite of due process of law."

The ruling mentioned "the failure of the trial court to make an effective appointment of counsel." The Court saw Roddy's and Moody's defense as just about as good as no defense at all.

The remaining Scottsboro Boys' convictions were reversed, but that did not mean that they were set free. It simply meant that the trial court's guilty verdicts were set aside, as if the trials had never taken place at all. It was now up to the state to decide whether to prosecute the cases again.

The state of Alabama chose to re-try the Scottsboro Boys, this time all together, confident that this time the prosecution would prevail. But toward the end of the retrial, one of the accusers, Ruby Bates, struck what looked like a fatal blow to the state's case. She took back her testimony. No one had raped her, she admitted. None of the defendants had touched or even spoken to her that day.

Despite Bates's dramatic testimony, a jury again found the defendants guilty as charged, and they were taken back to prison. But the state eventually dropped all charges against four of the seven and drove them out of Alabama to the Tennessee border, where they were released. The others remained behind bars, some for more than a decade. Finally, they all either escaped or were paroled.

Powell, which came four years before *Brown* v. *Mississippi*, marked the first time the U.S. Supreme Court had reversed a state court conviction because a defendant's due process rights had been violated. From then on, all states had to provide counsel for poor defendants in capital cases, where conviction could lead to death—but only in capital cases.

Betts v. Brady (1942)

The Court next dealt with the right to counsel in a 1942 case named *Betts* v. *Brady*. Petitioner Betts was an out-of-work farmhand when he was arrested in Carroll County, Maryland. Betts was poor, so he asked the trial court to appoint counsel for him. The judge told Betts that in Carroll County they appointed counsel for poor defendants only in cases of murder or rape, and Betts was charged with the lesser crime of robbery. So Betts had no choice but to defend himself as best he could.

It was not good enough. Betts was found guilty and sentenced to eight years behind bars. He took his case to state appeals courts and lost. Finally, unable to appeal to the state any longer, he petitioned the U.S. Supreme Court.

The Court accepted his petition because ten years earlier *Powell* had limited the right to counsel for poor defendants to capital cases only. *Powell* stated that "whether this would be so in other criminal prosecutions, or under other circumstances, we need not determine."

Now, the Court decided, it was time to make that determination: "The question we are now to decide is whether due process of law demands that in every criminal case, whatever the circumstances, a state must furnish counsel to an poor defendant."

To make their decision, the Court reviewed the constitutions of the individual states. The Court's study showed that most states did not order their courts to provide counsel for poor defendants. Therefore, the *Betts* decision said, "appointment of counsel is not a fundamental right, essential to a fair trial." And so, "In the light of this evidence we are unable to say that the concept of due process . . . obligates the states . . . to furnish counsel in every such case."

Betts lost and individual states remained free to decide whether to provide counsel in any cases except capital cases. The Court did, however, admit that under certain special circumstances, lawyers might be provided for defendants in noncapital cases. But the defense would first have to demonstrate that due process had been denied.

BLACK'S DISSENT

Betts was a 6 to 3 ruling. U.S. Supreme Court justices who are part of the minority may write dissenting opinions explaining why they disagree with the majority. Their dissents are not law, but they are published along with the majority opinion and may influence future decisions.

Justice Hugo Black was one of the three justices in the minority. In his *Betts* dissent, he wrote, "Whether a man is innocent cannot be determined from a trial in which, as here, denial of counsel has made it impossible to conclude, with any satisfactory degree of certainty, that the defendant's case was adequately presented."

In other words, we cannot be sure of a defendant's guilt or innocence if the defendant is not represented by counsel. Black went on to write of the need to "assure that no man shall be deprived of counsel merely because of his poverty. Any other practice seems to me to defeat the promise of our democratic society to provide equal justice under the law."

Black was still a justice three decades later, when the Court took up *Miranda* v. *Arizona*. But before then, Black would take part in two other landmark rulings in regard to the Sixth Amendment right to counsel. They came close together, two decades after *Betts*.

THE WARREN COURT

These two landmark rulings were *Gideon* v. *Wainwright* (1963) and *Escobedo* v. *Illinois* (1964). Together, the nine justices who took part in these rulings were known as the Warren Court. The name came from its Chief Justice, Earl Warren, whom President Dwight Eisenhower appointed Chief Justice in 1953.

The Warren Court lasted from 1953 to 1969. During those years it was known for taking an activist stance toward social and legal problems such as racial segregation, civil rights, separation of church and state—and suspects' rights. The Court made a number of rulings that shifted power from the government to the people.

Together, these rulings amounted to what historians call a "due process revolution." Using the due process clause of the Fourteenth Amendment, the Warren Court—for the first time in Court history—held the states responsible for guaranteeing citizens certain freedoms granted to them in the Bill of Rights.

Brown v. *Board of Education* (1954) is one of these rulings. Chief Justice Warren himself wrote the majority opinion in the unanimous ruling, telling the states that their long-standing tradition of racially segregated public schools was both unconstitutional and un-American.

These rulings put new checks and balances on government authorities, and that stirred up controversy. The Warren Court and its "due process revolution" rulings were liked by some people and disliked by others. Actually, *disliked* is probably too mild a word. During the 1960s, signs proclaiming **IMPEACH EARL WARREN** appeared on automobile bumpers and in people's yards

CHIEF JUSTICE EARL WARREN BECAME SO CONTROVERSIAL AS A RESULT OF SUCH ACTIVIST COURT DECISIONS AS *MIRANDA* THAT BILLBOARDS APPEARED THROUGHOUT THE SOUTH URGING THAT WARREN BE IMPEACHED.

and farm fields, especially in the deep South.

Because Supreme Court justices are appointed for life they cannot be fired. But they can be impeached—removed from office for misconduct. When Chief Justice Warren retired in 1969 some people were still calling for his impeachment. Some of this dislike came from the Court's rulings in cases such as *Gideon* v. *Wainwright* and *Escobedo* v. *Illinois*, which dealt with suspect's rights.

Gideon v. *Wainwright* (1963)

Like Betts, the defendant in *Gideon* v. *Wainwright* found himself in a bind. He did not have the money to hire a defense attorney, and the state would not appoint one for him. Clarence Earl Gideon, a poor drifter, was accused of stealing a small amount of money from a Panama City, Florida, poolroom. Here is the exchange between Gideon and the judge, referred to in this transcript as The COURT:

> The COURT: Mr. Gideon, I am sorry, but I cannot appoint Counsel to represent you in this case. Under the laws of the State of Florida, the only time the Court can appoint Counsel to represent a Defendant is when that person is charged with a capital offense. I am sorry, but I will have to deny

your request to appoint Counsel to defend you in this case.

The DEFENDANT: The United States Supreme Court says I am entitled to be represented by Counsel.

As we know from *Betts*, Gideon was mistaken. He was found guilty and sentenced to prison. He then appealed his case to the Florida State Supreme Court on the grounds that his conviction violated his Sixth Amendment rights under the U.S. Constitution. When his appeal was denied, he petitioned the U.S. Supreme Court. The Court accepted Gideon's petition because "the problem of a defendant's federal constitutional right to counsel in a state court has been a continuing source of controversy and litigation in both state and federal courts. To give this problem another review here, we granted [the cert petition]."

THE RULING

Justice Black delivered the majority opinion, which he wrote with the help of the other eight justices. The opinion includes several passages quoted from the Court's opinion in *Powell*. These passages help establish precedent. They help

CLARENCE EARL GIDEON, A POOR DRIFTER ACCUSED OF STEALING, MADE HISTORY WHEN *GIDEON* v. *WAINWRIGHT* WAS DECIDED IN HIS FAVOR BY THE SUPREME COURT. GIDEON ARGUED THAT HE LOST HIS CASE BECAUSE HE WAS DENIED THE RIGHT TO COUNSEL.

show that the Court's ruling is solidly grounded in rulings from past cases.

What would it be like to be in Gideon's place? Justice Black had this question firmly in mind when he quoted this passage from *Powell*, which he himself helped write three decades earlier: "Even the intelligent and educated layman has small and sometimes no skill in the science of law. If charged with a crime, he is incapable, generally, of determining for himself whether the indictment is good or bad. He is unfamiliar with the rules of evidence. Left without the aid of counsel . . . he lacks both the skill and

ASSOCIATE JUSTICE HUGO L. BLACK WROTE THE MAJORITY OPINION IN *GIDEON* v. *WAINWRIGHT*. SINCE THAT TIME, THE POOR HAVE GAINED THE RIGHT TO FREE LEGAL COUNSEL.

knowledge adequately to prepare his defense, even though he have a perfect one."

Black described the powerful forces arrayed against Gideon: "Governments, both state and federal, quite properly spend vast sums of money to establish machinery to try defendants accused of crime. Lawyers to prosecute are everywhere deemed essential to protect the public's interest in an orderly society."

Black also quotes this passage from *Powell* to show the danger of false convictions: "He [the defendant] requires the guiding hand of counsel at every step in the proceedings against him. Without it, though he be not guilty, he faces the danger of conviction because he does not know how to establish his innocence."

Black wrote that Gideon defended himself about as well as could be expected from a man who knew so little about criminal law. Gideon made an opening statement to the jury and cross-examined the prosecution's witnesses. He went on to present his own defense and to close with an argument that emphasized his innocence of the charges against him. Still, the jury brought back a verdict of guilty, and Gideon was sentenced to five years in Florida state prison.

THE RESULTS

Near the end of the *Gideon* ruling, Justice Black wrote that "in our adversary system of criminal justice, any person haled into court, who is too poor to hire a lawyer, cannot be assured a fair trial unless counsel is provided for him." Our noble ideal that every defendant stands equal before the law "cannot be realized if the poor man charged with a crime has to face his accusers without a lawyer to assist him."

The *Gideon* ruling ended by overruling a decision Black had opposed as a member of the Court two decades earlier. "The Court in *Betts* v. *Brady* departed from the sound wisdom upon which the Court's holding in *Powell* v. *Alabama* rested," the opinion declared, and *Betts* "should now be overruled."

Powell (1932) required that a lawyer be appointed for poor defendants in state cases charged with a capital crime. *Betts* (1942) refused to extend that right to defendants accused of lesser crimes. Now *Gideon* (1963) extended that right of counsel to felony cases, where the defendant faces a year or more in jail.

The *Gideon* ruling came in March 1963. Three months later *The New York Times* conducted a survey to measure the effects. It found that state legislatures were rewriting their laws to go along with the ruling. Cities and counties without public defender's offices were opening them, hiring lawyers the court could appoint and pay to defend poor defendants.

And Gideon himself? His case was sent back for retrial, and this time he was acquitted and released. Gideon remained a drifter but kept out of trouble with the law. He died penniless in 1972 at the age of sixty-one.

But before his death, Gideon would see the legal trend he had influenced carried further, with criminal suspects securing more and better protections under the law. The next big change in this trend came a year after the *Gideon* ruling, with another U.S. Supreme Court decision that would strongly influence *Miranda*.

ESCOBEDO V. *ILLINOIS* (1964)

Escobedo was another case that focused on a defendant's right to counsel, but with a different twist. Instead of *whether* a poor defendant had a right to counsel, it was all about *when*.

DANIEL ESCOBEDO WAS ARRESTED FOR MURDER, BUT HIS CONVICTION WAS
OVERTURNED BY THE SUPREME COURT, WHICH RULED THAT THOSE ARRESTED
ARE ENTITLED TO LEGAL REPRESENTATION BEFORE THE POLICE CAN BEGIN
AN INTERROGATION.

On the night of January 19, 1960, in Chicago, Illinois,
a man was fatally shot. At 2:30 the next morning, a suspect
was arrested and charged with the shooting. He was Daniel
Escobedo, a twenty-two-year-old Mexican American with
a history of brushes with the law.

Escobedo was interrogated by police but gave no
statement. Police released him at 5 AM when they received
a writ of *habeas corpus* obtained by Escobedo's lawyer. A
writ of habeas corpus is an order that forces police to
either charge a suspect or release him.

Then, on January 30, another suspect in police custody, Benedict DiGerlando, told police that Escobedo had fired the fatal shots.

Escobedo was arrested again, handcuffed, and driven to police headquarters. On the way, the arresting officers told him what DiGerlando had said. You might as well confess, they told Escobedo. But instead, Escobedo said, "I am sorry but I would like to have advice from my lawyer."

THE INTERROGATION

At headquarters, Escobedo was taken to an interrogation room. According to one of the arresting officers, Escobedo was in custody and knew that he "couldn't walk out the door."

Not long after that, Escobedo's lawyer, Warren Wolfson, arrived at police headquarters and asked to see his client. To Wolfson's surprise, police refused. One officer testified that he told Wolfson he could not see Escobedo until they were through interrogating him.

During this time, Escobedo asked to see Wolfson several times, and Wolfson did the same. But police refused their requests. Wolfson remained in the building but saw his client only once, by accident. "[F]or a second or two I spotted him in an office in the Homicide Bureau," Wolfson said. "The door was open and I could see through the office. . . . I waved to him and he waved back and then the door was closed, by one of the officers at Homicide."

Wolfson would not give up. "I had a conversation with every police officer I could find," he said. "I quoted to Captain Flynn the Section of the [Illinois] Criminal Code which allows an attorney the right to see his client." Wolfson stayed until 1:00 AM before finally going home.

Meanwhile, police kept interrogating Escobedo. An officer testified that during the interrogation, DiGerlando and Escobedo were brought into the same room to confront each other, and Escobedo told DiGerlando that he was lying. "I didn't shoot [the victim]," Escobedo said. "You did it."

At this point Escobedo admitted that he was involved in the killing. He was then taken to another interrogation room. Police kept him handcuffed and on his feet as they interrogated him for another four hours.

Escobedo testified that one of the officers, Montejano, spoke to him in Spanish and told him that he could go home. All he had to do was pin the murder on his alleged accomplice, DiGerlando. If Escobedo would do this, police would not hold him responsible for the shooting in any way. Escobedo said that he confessed only because of what Montejano told him. Montejano disagreed. He never offered the suspect any kind of deal or any such assurance, he testified.

One thing all parties did agree on, though: At no time was Escobedo advised of his right to remain silent or allowed to see his lawyer.

Despite Escobedo's objections, his confession was admitted into evidence and used against him at his trial, and he was convicted of murder. Escobedo appealed his conviction to the Illinois State Supreme Court. His confession should have been excluded, he insisted, since he was denied a lawyer during interrogation. His appeal failed. Finally, as a last resort, he appealed to the U.S. Supreme Court.

THE *ESCOBEDO* RULING

As we know from *Gideon*, a defendant in a felony or capital case was already entitled to a lawyer at the time of trial, even if he could not pay for one. Now, in *Escobedo*, the petitioner was asking that this right be extended to the time of interrogation.

The Court agreed with the petitioner. The Court's ruling in *Escobedo* v. *Illinois* (1964) held that the accused had been denied the assistance of counsel in violation of the Sixth Amendment. Because of this, no statement made during interrogation could be used against him at a criminal trial. His trial court conviction was reversed.

In the *Miranda* ruling two years later, the Court would emphasize how a lawyer can help lessen the unfair advantage that police hold over a suspect. This statement from *Miranda* applies to *Escobedo* as well: "The presence of an attorney, and the warnings delivered to the individual, enable the defendant . . . to tell his story without fear, effectively, and in a way that eliminates the evils in the interrogation process."

And so *Escobedo* took a criminal suspect's rights a step beyond where *Gideon* had taken them. From now on, a suspect accused of a felony or a capital crime had the right to have an attorney present when police questioned him.

REACTING TO *ESCOBEDO*

Escobedo was a 5 to 4 decision. Justice Byron R. White, one of the four minority justices, wrote a dissent to the majority opinion. "The decision is thus another major step in the direction of the goal which the Court seemingly has in mind—to bar from evidence all admissions obtained from an individual suspected of crime, whether involuntarily made or not," White wrote.

In other words, White thought the Court had gone too far in its mission to strengthen a suspect's rights. The Court was now doing serious harm to the U.S. criminal justice system, he argued.

Associate Justice Byron R. White wrote the dissent in the *Escobedo* decision. He felt that the Court had gone too far in protecting the rights of criminals.

Would *Escobedo* lead to what White had predicted—an end to confessions as evidence, voluntary and involuntary alike? Orlando Wilson was head of the Chicago police force that arrested and interrogated Escobedo. In May 1966, Chief Wilson declared that *Escobedo* violated common sense and made things more difficult for law enforcement officers.

One of Ernesto Miranda's attorneys, John P. Frank, reacted to Wilson's criticism: "We have not taken the position that there cannot be voluntary confessions, but we have taken the position that, by God, the poor are entitled to be told of their right to counsel before it's too late."

State courts also reacted to *Escobedo*. They were legally bound to honor the ruling, but they were also free to interpret it in different ways. Some lower court judges interpreted the ruling broadly. To them, *Escobedo* meant that the accused must have a lawyer in the interrogation room unless he or she specifically waives, or gives up, that right.

Other judges took a narrow approach. Only suspects who actually asked for a lawyer during interrogation, as Escobedo had, would get one. If the accused did not ask, then the interrogation could proceed, and all statements were admissible in court, as long as they were voluntary. As we shall see, the Arizona State Supreme Court took this narrow approach when they denied Miranda's appeal at the state level.

WHAT MAKES A CONFESSION VOLUNTARY?

Criminal law is never absolute. It evolves, changing year by year. Most of the U.S. Supreme Court decisions discussed so far, from *Brown* v. *Mississippi* (1936) to *Escobedo* (1964), kept broadening criminal suspects' protections when it came to the right to remain silent and the right to counsel.

But these protections differed from state to state. There was no uniform standard for what made a confession voluntary. It was still up to state courts to decide whether the defendant's due process rights had been violated, using the *totality-of-circumstances* standard. This standard assumes that no single factor should determine whether a confession was voluntary and not coerced. Instead, several factors must be taken into account, including the defendant's age, intelligence, education, any earlier run-ins with the law, and any coercive tactics that police officers might have used, such as physical brutality or long periods of questioning without food or sleep.

State courts would consider all these factors when evaluating a confession. This totality-of-circumstances approach left a great deal of room for subjective judgment. As a result, a court in one state might rule a confession voluntary while a court in another state might rule the very same confession involuntary and coerced.

Advocates for suspects' rights called this totality-of-circumstances approach arbitrary, uncertain, and unfair. Among suspects' rights advocates were two of the *Miranda* justices, Hugo Black and William O. Douglas. Both spoke out for reform. The Court was now ready to take up a case about setting uniform standards for what made a confession voluntary and not coerced, and *Miranda* v. *Arizona* would be that case.

Chief Justice Earl Warren presided over many cases that changed the law of the land forever, but he did not decide them alone; the majority of the justices had to agree to take an activist stance.

four
FILING THE CASE

THE FIRST STEP in getting a case to the Supreme Court is to ask for a review. A request for review comes in the form of a *writ of certiorari*, or *cert* for short. A cert is a written petition filed by the loser in the lower courts. It asks the Court to review the lower court decision in hopes of getting the verdict reversed.

What are the chances of having a cert accepted? The Court is in session about nine months of the year. During that time it receives thousands of certs. Some are put together by legal professionals. Others are written by prisoners, the ones who can't afford to pay a lawyer. Some of these come from inmates who have studied the law in prison. They are neat and formal, carefully typed, using proper legal language. Others are neither neat nor formal. They may be written out by hand in pen, pencil, or even crayon on lined notebook paper.

Since the Court receives so many certs and can handle so few, granting of cert is rare. The Court typically dismisses 99 percent of the petitions it receives without discussion. The remaining certs are reviewed, and if four or more of the nine justices vote yes, the Court accepts the appeal. To be accepted, the cert must give the Court "compelling reasons" for review.

THE RIGHT REASONS

The Court publishes a guide defining these compelling reasons. It says the petition must focus on "an important federal question"—a question involving possible violations of the U.S. Constitution. Miranda claimed that his Fifth and Sixth Amendment rights under the U.S. Constitution had been violated.

Miranda could not pay his trial lawyer to petition the Court. He had no money, and Moore could not afford to freely give the time it would take to research and write the petition.

Miranda needed help, and he got it from the American Civil Liberties Union (ACLU). This national organization is dedicated to defending people's constitutional rights. This includes the rights of people like Miranda, who are serving jail time for violent crimes.

Miranda's case came to the ACLU's attention, and their lawyers contacted John J. Flynn at the Phoenix law firm of Lewis & Roca to help. Some U.S. law firms take on a few cases each year on a *pro bono* (free) basis. It's a tradition among these firms to give some of their time and resources to help poor defendants and prisoners. Flynn would work with John P. Frank, also of Lewis & Roca. A U.S. Supreme Court appeal was an expensive matter. The *Miranda* appeal would cost the firm an estimated $50,000 in office time alone.

What made Ernesto Miranda deserving of such highly skilled and expensive help? It was not the man himself; it was the important constitutional rights involved. As the U.S. Supreme Court guide said, Miranda's case involved "an important federal question." Flynn and Frank saw a chance to argue a case before the U.S. Supreme Court, an achievement that many lawyers dream about but few ever see come true.

THE SIXTH AMENDMENT ARGUMENT

Actually, Miranda's case involved two important federal questions. Both the Fifth Amendment right to remain silent and the Sixth Amendment right to counsel were at stake, as they were in *Escobedo*. But Frank and Flynn wanted to limit their argument to keep it tightly focused. So they decided to stick with the Sixth Amendment right to counsel. The Arizona State Supreme Court had deprived Miranda of this precious right, they said, by interpreting the *Escobedo* ruling too narrowly.

Miranda was in serious need of counsel at the interrogation stage, they wrote in their cert. True, he had not expressly asked for counsel when the police took him into Interrogation Room #2. If the police had advised Miranda of his Sixth Amendment right to counsel and if he had waived it, that would be different.

But Miranda was never advised of his rights, so he had no opportunity to accept or waive them. In some states police would have had to advise Miranda before interrogating him, but not the state of Arizona. The *Miranda* cert asked the Court to review the case "so that the current widely conflicting treatment of a basic constitutional right [to counsel] can be resolved, and substantial and similar justice attained by all accused persons wherever they live."

As it turned out, Frank and Flynn had made the right argument at the right time. The justices were more than ready to deal with the important federal questions raised in the *Miranda* cert. They were eager. Six months after their June 1964 *Escobedo* ruling, the justices ordered their law clerks to start setting aside and summarizing any certs based on *Escobedo* issues.

By November 1965, when the justices discussed the *Miranda* cert, they had summaries of 150 other certs from twenty-five different states, all addressing questions of constitutional law raised in *Escobedo*. There was no doubt in the justices' minds that the time had come to deal with these issues.

FOUR CASES IN ONE

But which certs would they choose? The Court often rolls several cases into one. This time the justices chose four. One was *Miranda* v. *Arizona*. The others were *Vignera* v. *New York*, *Westover* v. *United States*, and *California* v. *Stewart*. Because *Miranda* was filed first, the four appeals were decided together under the single name *Miranda* v. *Arizona*.

The justices were careful of which certs they chose. They wanted cases that dealt with the right to remain silent and the right to counsel, but they did not want cases where the defendants had committed acts of extreme violence against victims or where the police had brutalized suspects. That way the justices could more easily focus on Constitutional questions in making their decisions.

In *Vignera*, Michael Vignera was arrested and taken to police headquarters, where he was questioned about a Brooklyn, New York, dress shop robbery. Eventually, Vignera admitted to the robbery and signed a written confession. At no time did police notify him of his right to counsel. At the trial, the judge told the jury, "The law doesn't say that the confession is void or invalidated because the police officer didn't advise the defendant as to his rights." Vignera was found guilty. Since he was a repeat offender, he was sentenced to thirty to sixty years in prison.

In *Westover*, Carl Calvin Westover was arrested in Kansas City, Missouri, on suspicion of two California robberies. First, the Kansas City police interrogated him. They did not advise him of his right to remain silent or his right to counsel. Then the FBI questioned

Westover. But first the officers advised him of his rights. Westover then confessed to both robberies and signed written confessions. He was tried in federal court and sentenced to fifteen years in prison for each robbery.

In *California* v. *Stewart*, the defendant, Roy Allen Stewart, was interrogated repeatedly about a series of purse-snatchings. In one of them, the victim had died of injuries inflicted by her assailant. When police searched Stewart's house, they found items connecting him to the robberies. Police questioned Stewart on nine occasions over a five-day period. During that time he was kept in a prison cell and never advised of his right to counsel.

At the ninth session, Stewart confessed to robbing and killing one of the victims. His confession was used as evidence in his trial, and he was found guilty and sentenced to death.

But on appeal to the California State Supreme Court, Stewart's conviction was reversed. Because of *Escobedo*, the court ruled, Stewart should have been advised of his right to remain silent and of his right to counsel. This was the only one of the four cases in which the state, and not the defendant, was the petitioner.

WHAT THE cases had in common

The focus of the four cases was clear and sharp. All dealt with the same question: Could police legally obtain a confession from a suspect without first advising him of his Fifth Amendment right to remain silent and his Sixth Amendment right to counsel? The Court summed them up this way:

> In each of these cases the defendant while in police custody was questioned . . . in a room in which

he was cut off from the outside world. None of the defendants was given a full and effective warning of his rights at the outset of the interrogation process. In all four cases the questioning [produced oral confessions], and in three of them signed statements as well, which were admitted at their trials. All defendants were convicted and all convictions, except in [*California* v. *Stewart*], were affirmed on appeal. . . . They all thus share [important] features—[secret] interrogation of individuals in a police-dominated atmosphere, resulting in self-incriminating statements without full warnings of constitutional rights.

THe PeTITIONer's BrIeF

After cert is granted, the petitioner must file a brief with the Court. A brief is a longer and more detailed version of the cert. It tells why the lower-court decision should be reversed. It also lays the foundation for the oral argument that the petitioner will present to the Court in the next step.

Frank and Flynn's *Miranda* brief carefully traced the evolution of the law governing a criminal suspect's right to counsel, from *Powell* v. *Alabama* (1932) to *Escobedo* v. *Illinois* (1964). The brief argued that based on these rulings, Miranda's confession should have been excluded from evidence in the lower-court trial, and so the Court should reverse the lower-court conviction.

The petitioner's brief was filed with the Court on January 19, 1966. A copy immediately went to the respondent, the state of Arizona, which had several weeks' time to respond with its own brief, telling why the lower-court decision should stand.

THE RESPONDENT'S BRIEF

The respondent's brief for the state of Arizona was filed by Gary K. Nelson, assistant attorney general in charge of the Arizona Criminal Appeals Division. Nelson's argument focused on the differences between the *Miranda* and *Escobedo* cases. The Phoenix police had not made the mistakes that got the Chicago police into trouble in the *Escobedo* case, Nelson insisted. While Chicago police had kept Escobedo from talking with his lawyer, Phoenix police had never denied Miranda counsel. How could they, when he never asked to see a lawyer?

Nelson wrote that a suspect's confession should not be suppressed "unless that evidence is determined not to be the product of the free and uncoerced will of the accused, or if it is obtained after the police have [denied] the accused his rights to counsel." And while Chicago police had never informed Escobedo of his legal right to counsel, Miranda had signed a paper stating that he confessed "with full knowledge of my legal rights, understanding any statement I make may be used against me."

THE ACLU BRIEF

The nine U.S. Supreme Court justices each received a copy of both briefs to study before the oral argument stage began. It was scheduled for the week of February 28, 1966. In the meantime, more briefs were filed. These were *amicus curiae*, or friend of the court, briefs. Individuals or groups who are vitally interested in a case may file amicus curiae briefs, arguing for the petitioner or respondent. Justices receive copies to read and may be influenced by the arguments they present.

The ACLU filed an amicus curiae brief in support of the petitioner. It looked at the case through the eyes of the suspect. The brief included quotes from police manuals used to teach police the techniques commonly used to pressure suspects into confessing. Here, from the ACLU brief, are two of these interrogation techniques. The first is called "strategic interruptions":

> When the interrogator senses that he is losing control or that his tactics are availing nothing, it may be time to pause and do additional planning or introduce a new technique. The interrogation room should be equipped with a button and buzzer under the top of the desk, which the investigator can push with his knee or foot. In this way, he can sound the buzzer, pretend it is a signal for him and leave the room.

This second technique, known as "jolting," is designed to pressure the suspect more strongly:

> The questioning is conducted at some length in a quiet, almost soothing manner. By constantly observing the suspect, the investigator chooses [the right] moment to shout a pertinent question and appear as though he is beside himself with rage. The subject may be unnerved to the extent of confessing. If he appears moved, the interrogator will work him up to a pitch with a climactic series of questions.

Neither technique uses physical brutality. Both— especially the second—aim to manipulate the suspect psychologically, or "get into his head." They play parts in a plan meant to pressure him into confessing. The ACLU brief objects to these pressure tactics on constitutional grounds. It claims they violate "the subject's right not to be compelled to incriminate himself." The ACLU brief goes on to say this about police interrogation techniques in general: "Their basic attitude is one of getting the subject to confess despite himself—by trapping him into it, by deceiving him, or by more direct means of [breaking down] his will."

Briefs supporting the Respondent

Two law enforcement groups filed amicus curiae briefs in support of the state of Arizona. The National District Attorneys Association looked at things through the eyes of law enforcement officers. It warned that extending the right to counsel to the interrogation stage would make it harder for them to obtain voluntary confessions.

The other amicus brief was filed on behalf of the attorneys general of more than half the fifty states. The state attorney general is the chief law officer of a state. This brief looked at the situation as a clash between state and federal government. It asked the Court to leave matters of law enforcement at the state level to state lawmakers. It said state courts should be allowed to make and enforce their own rules for dealing with suspects, and that included the duty of protecting suspects from abuse by law enforcement officers. In other words, the U.S. Supreme Court should stay out of the state courts' affairs and allow the Arizona trial court's guilty verdict in the *Miranda* case stand.

The briefs were filed and read. On the morning of February 28, 1966, the next stage of *Miranda* v. *Arizona* was set to begin.

FIVE
THE ORAL ARGUMENTS

THE UNITED STATES SUPREME COURT building
is located at One First Street, NE, across First Street from
the U.S. Capitol and across East Capitol Street from the
Library of Congress. It is a majestic structure, measuring
385 feet by 304 feet. It was built to symbolize the national
ideal of justice in its highest and purest form, solid and
shining outside and in. Outside, the principal material is
marble from U.S. quarries in Vermont, Georgia, and
Alabama. Inside, the doors, trim, paneled walls, and many
of the floors are made from American quartered oak, a
rich and solid wood.

The courtroom itself, where the oral arguments take
place, is decorated by marble pillars. At the front is the
bench where the justices sit, elevated on a platform
and backed by red velour curtains.

Court begins promptly at 10 AM. That's when the crier,
the court official who shouts out announcements,
smashes down the gavel. Instantly everyone in the room
rises, and the crier calls out: "The Honorable, the Chief
Justice and the Associate Justices of the Supreme Court of
the United States!"

The curtains part and the nine justices walk in and
take their places at the bench. "All persons having
business before the Honorable, the Supreme Court of

the United States, are admonished to draw near and give their attention, for the Court is now sitting," the crier continues. "God save the United States and this Honorable Court!"

THE PETITIONER'S POSITION

Now the oral arguments were set to begin. The nine justices already knew what to expect. After giving the *Miranda* brief a thorough reading, they saw where the petitioner's argument stood. Clearly, his argument would focus on the Sixth Amendment right to counsel.

As we know, the petitioner's brief began by reviewing the landmark cases leading up to *Miranda*. "We deal here with growing law, and look to where we are going by considering where we have been. . . . The Court in *Powell* (1936) recognized that the right to counsel was a growing, not a static constitutional right." In other words, with *Powell* the right to counsel moved toward becoming a federal law applying to all states equally.

However, the brief continued, that progress came to a sudden halt with *Betts* v. *Brady* (1942). In *Betts*, the Court ruled that while the federal government did have to provide an attorney for poor defendants in any and all cases, state governments did not. "The case held . . . that while counsel was required in capital cases and in some undefined other cases, it was not required in all cases."

Therefore, *Betts* failed to answer the vital constitutional question of "whether Sixth Amendment principles should in fact be imported into the interpretation of the Fourteenth Amendment" and apply to the individual states as well as the federal government.

Then the brief moved ahead twenty-one years to *Gideon* v. *Wainwright* (1963), where the law was applied more broadly. *Gideon* "erased the fundamental distinction between the state and federal cases by holding that Sixth Amendment guarantee of counsel . . . applied to the states in full." Thanks to *Gideon*, the Sixth Amendment now applied to the states as well as the federal government.

Finally came the *Escobedo* ruling. It stated that "when the process shifts from investigatory to accusatory—when its focus is on the accused and its purpose is to elicit a confession . . . the accused must be permitted to consult with his lawyer."

However, the *Miranda* brief stated, "We cannot [say] that *Escobedo* (1964) . . . establishes a right to counsel at the interrogation stage in all situations." The petitioner, Miranda, was asking that the right be extended to "all situations," including his own.

THE QUESTION OF WHEN

Frank and Flynn's brief moved on to the specific constitutional question facing the Court: Was a poor suspect entitled to the services of a lawyer during the interrogation stage, whether he asked for one or not?

Frank and Flynn's answer was yes. To support this position, they turned to the writings of one of the justices who would be hearing their argument, Justice William O. Douglas. Douglas had made strong statements about suspects' rights in earlier Court rulings, and the brief quoted some of these: "[W]hat takes place in the secret confines of the police station may be more critical than what takes place at the trial." And, "[A]ny accused—whether rich or poor—has the right to consult a lawyer before talking with the police." Douglas also had said that a lawyer during interrogation was most important to "the poor, the ignorant, and frequently, those of limited mental ability."

The brief also addressed the question of increased

costs, since states would have to hire more public defenders for poor suspects: "The right to counsel under public defender systems may well be costly, but the dollar cost of preservation of a constitutional right is no reason for ignoring that right."

How did this right to counsel apply specifically to Ernesto Miranda? The brief went on to explain:

When this defendant [Miranda] went into Interrogation Room 2, instead of having "the guiding hand of counsel" to which we believe the principles of *Powell* v. *Alabama* entitled him, he had the guiding hand of two policemen. When he came out of Interrogation Room 2, there was no longer any point in giving him counsel—his case was over. We believe that such practices are barred by the Sixth and Fourteenth Amendments to the Constitution of the United States.

The brief ended by recalling how the law in regard to a suspect's right to counsel had advanced since the days of the Star Chamber: "This is not the result of a single case, *Escobedo* or any other. Rather, there is a tide in the affairs of men, and it is this engulfing tide which is washing away the secret interrogation of the unprotected accused."

THE RESPONDENT'S POSITION
Gary K. Nelson's brief for the state of Arizona looked at things from the opposite direction. While the *Miranda* brief asked the Court to expand the limits of the right to an attorney, the state asked that the limits remain right where *Escobedo* had left them.

And where was that? The *Escobedo* ruling said that a criminal suspect had the right to an attorney during interrogation if he requested one. Daniel Escobedo had asked, and the police had said no, and that was a clear violation of his Sixth Amendment right.

But Miranda had never asked for an attorney.

And why had the Phoenix police not informed him of his right to ask for one? Not because they were trying to deny him that right, Nelson wrote. Miranda was already aware of that right, as well as the right to remain silent. How could the police have known this? Nelson quoted from the Arizona State Supreme Court ruling:

> [Miranda's police record] included being arrested in California on suspicion of armed robbery, and a conviction and sentence in Tennessee. . . . His experience under previous cases would indicate that his statement that he understood his rights was true. . . . [W]e hold that . . . defendant's constitutional rights were not violated, and it was proper to admit the statement in evidence."

Therefore, Nelson argued, Miranda's right to counsel under *Escobedo* had clearly not been violated. So, to win his appeal, Miranda had asked the Court to take that right a step further and expand it. Miranda wanted the justices to rule that not informing a criminal suspect of his right to an attorney was itself a violation of that right. And Nelson's brief argued that the Court should deny this request.

The respondent's brief also took up this question: Were Miranda's statements during interrogation truly voluntary? It quoted from Miranda's handwritten confession: "Seen a girl walking up street stopped a little ahead of her got out of car walked towards her grabbed her by the arm and asked to get in the car. Got in car without force tied hands & ankles. Drove away for a few miles."

Miranda's confession went on to describe the rape in the desert. Clearly, he had voluntarily confessed to the crime, the brief said. And that confession included a statement admitting that Miranda knew his constitutional rights. So there was no reason for the lower court to exclude the confession from evidence.

MIRANDA WAS NOT THE VICTIM

And what about Miranda's claim that the police had ruined his life? Nelson responded: "Petitioner states that his life for all practical purposes was over when he walked out of Interrogation Room #2 on March 13, 1963. The real fact is that Miranda's life was unalterably destined ten days earlier during the late evening hours of March 2 and the early morning hours of March 3, when he kidnapped and raped his victim . . . ."

In other words, the young woman Miranda assaulted was the victim in this case, not the criminal who confessed to assaulting her. Committing a violent crime is what landed Miranda in prison, not the lack of a lawyer during questioning. Nelson wrote: "[T]he intent of the Constitutional safeguards were to insure, as much as humanly possible, that the innocent and unpopular would not be wrongfully harassed, intimidated or convicted—not that the guilty should have any special chances for acquittal or other favorable result."

Nelson's brief went on to hammer this point home:

If the prosecuting authorities have gained an overwhelming advantage over a particular defendant, assuming they have done so by proper

methods, and not by violating any of his constitutional rights, this is to be highly commended, not
condemned. . . . There is not "gamesmanship" or
"sportsmanship" involved here, at least insofar as
the criminal is concerned. He follows no code of
conduct or canons of ethics.

Nelson also reminded the Court of the seriousness of
violent crime: "The death, suffering, and depravation . . .
is as real to those who are touched by its sting as is that of
any war ever fought. Certainly the criminal gives no
quarter; and none should be given in return except as is
required to insure the integrity and continuation of the
system which we all cherish."
He concluded the state's brief with these words:

If a criminal has been clever in the commission of
his crime, but is foolish or careless in his handling
of the police interrogation of him concerning that
crime, the evidence obtained as a result . . . should
not be suppressed unless that evidence is determined not to be the product of the free will of the
accused, or if it is obtained after the police have
undertaken a course of conduct calculated to deny
the accused his right to counsel.

SHIFTING GEARS

In the oral arguments stage, the lawyer for the petitioner
speaks first. He faces the justices from in front of the
bench where they sit, looking down at him. Flynn delivered the oral argument for *Miranda*. He proceeded
through the main points in the brief as the nine black-
robed justices listened. But he was interrupted often. The
justices may interrupt during oral arguments whenever

they wish. The interruption is usually a question or comment that challenges the lawyer or asks for clarification.

Sometimes the justices' questions lead the lawyer to shift gears and change the plan of attack. This happened to Flynn. Remember that the petitioner's brief was based on the Sixth Amendment right to counsel. From the justices' questions, Flynn saw that they were just as concerned with the Fifth Amendment right to remain silent.

So Flynn started arguing his points in terms of both rights. By failing to inform Miranda of his right to counsel *and* his right to remain silent, Flynn insisted, the Phoenix police had denied Miranda both of these basic constitutional rights.

Then Nelson argued his case for the state of Arizona, proceeding through his brief from point to point, interrupted along the way by questions from the nine justices. The oral arguments were complete on March 1, 1966.

MAKING UP THEIR MINDS

Now it was time for the justices to thoughtfully consider all that they had read and heard in the written briefs and oral arguments for both sides, and then come to a decision.

Some U.S. Supreme Court decisions are based on interpreting the Constitution, which one political commentator has called that "strange, ambiguous, open-to-interpretation document." While many government documents attempt to be precise, the Constitution is deliberately general and vague. It is meant to serve as an enduring foundation, but a foundation only. It is meant to be interpreted. Some U.S. Supreme Court decisions represent a significant new interpretation of some part of the U.S. Constitution, and *Miranda* was destined to be one of these.

Interpretations are personal matters, and each of the Court's decisions is influenced by the Court's makeup. The justices all look at things from their own personal point of view. They all apply their own unique sets of beliefs and feelings to the constitutional questions in any given decision.

Some justices are known as strict constructionists. They tend to be conservative when it comes to interpreting the Constitution. If, in their opinion, the answer to a question before the Court is not contained in the Constitution, then that question must be left to the judgment of state and federal legislators. Justice Antonin Scalia expressed the strict constructionist point of view in this quote from his dissent to a 1998 Court opinion: "We go beyond our proper role as judges in a democratic society when we restrict the people's power to govern themselves over the full range of policy choices that the Constitution has left available to them."

In the *Miranda* case, a strict constructionist would be more likely to rule against the petitioner. After all, the Fifth and Sixth Amendments never specifically mention a criminal suspect's right to counsel during interrogation. Yet Miranda was asking the Court to expand that right.

Other justices are known as progressives or activists. They tend to be more liberal in interpreting the Constitution, but only as long as these interpretations reflect what they see as the Founding Fathers' vision for the nation. These activist justices would be more likely to favor the petitioner in *Miranda*.

Miranda was asking the Court to strengthen the rights of the individual to protect him from the power the government may use against him. This activist attitude belongs to a tradition that dates back more than three centuries, to John Lilburn's denunciation at the Court of the Star Chamber.

THE WARREN COURT

The makeup of the Warren Court indicates the way each of these nine justices was likely to vote. A number of the Warren Court's rulings ended up in a 5 to 4 split. This showed how deeply divided the Court was between activists and constructionists.

THE SUPREME COURT JUSTICES WHO DECIDED *MIRANDA*, FROM LEFT TO RIGHT, STANDING: ASSOCIATE JUSTICES BYRON R. WHITE, WILLIAM J. BRENNAN JR., POTTER STEWART, AND TOM C. CLARK. SEATED: ASSOCIATE JUSTICES HUGO L. BLACK AND ABE FORTAS, CHIEF JUSTICE EARL WARREN, ASSOCIATE JUSTICES WILLIAM O. DOUGLAS AND JOHN M. HARLAN.

The four justices who generally voted as activists were Hugo L. Black, William O. Douglas, William J. Brennan Jr., and Chief Justice Earl Warren. When it came to suspects'-rights issues, the four tended to see things more through the eyes of the suspect than the police. All four were expected to vote in favor of Miranda.

The four justices who generally voted as strict constructionists were John M. Harlan, Tom C. Clark, Potter Stewart, and Byron R. White. In terms of suspects'-rights issues, they tended to see things more through the eyes of the police than the suspect. They were expected to vote for the respondent, against Miranda.

If predictions were right, this meant a vote of 4 to 4, a deadlock between activists and constructionists. Who would break it?

THE NINTH JUSTICE

The ninth justice was Abe Fortas, recently appointed by President Lyndon Johnson. One question was on the mind of everyone concerned with *Miranda*: How would Fortas vote?

With only seven months on the Court, his voting record was too small to give much of a sign. That left his career before becoming a justice to predict how he would vote. Like all justices, Fortas had been a lawyer. In fact, he was the one who argued *Gideon* v. *Wainwright* before the Court just two years earlier.

Fortas had argued successfully for the petitioner. In his oral argument he revealed how he felt about the question of a poor suspect's rights:

> I do believe that in some of this Court's decisions there has been a tendency . . . to forget the realities of what happens downstairs, of what happens to these poor, miserable, poor people when they are arrested and they are brought into the jail and

they are questioned and later on they are brought in these strange and awesome circumstances before a [judge].

After thoroughly discussing the case as presented by the petitioner and the respondent, the justices voted. By tradition, the most junior justice voted first. That way his decision would not be influenced by those of the senior judges. The most junior justice was Fortas. Then the other justices voted, in order of seniority, with Chief Justice Warren voting last.

The decision would affect a great many people's lives, not just at the time of the decision but far into the future as well. The Court's ruling in *Miranda* would become a matter of public policy. It would influence how police interrogations were carried out in all fifty states for many years to come.

ASSOCIATE JUSTICE ABE FORTAS HAD JUST BEEN APPOINTED BEFORE *MIRANDA* WAS DECIDED. HIS VOTE IN FAVOR OF ERNESTO MIRANDA TURNED THE TIDE IN THAT DECISION.

CHIEF JUSTICE EARL WARREN CHOSE TO WRITE THE *MIRANDA* DECISION HIM-
SELF, SO STRONGLY DID HE FEEL.

SIX
THE RULING

WHAT WAS THE VOTE?

The many people anxiously waiting for the final word on *Miranda* would have to wait a while longer. The decision in a U.S. Supreme Court case is not announced until the opinions are written.

The majority opinion is the one that counts most. It both announces the Court's decision and explains the reasoning behind it. These opinions tend to be tens of thousands of words long. Creating one takes weeks and sometimes months of research, discussion, writing, revising, arguing, and re-revising before all the majority justices can agree on the exact wording throughout.

The majority opinion is a cooperative effort but it does have a single author. The Chief Justice selects the author, provided the Chief Justice has voted with the majority. If not, then the senior justice on the majority side, the one with the most years on the Court, does the choosing.

Chief Justice Earl Warren chose himself to write the *Miranda* opinion. It was no surprise that he, along with the other activist justices—Brennan, Black, and Douglas— voted with the majority. Nor was it a surprise that the four justices known for being strict constructionists—Harlan, Clark, White, and Stewart—made up the minority.

The only justice whose vote was at all uncertain was

Abe Fortas, and it was his vote in favor of Ernesto Miranda that made the petitioner the winner. Ernesto Miranda won his appeal 5 to 4. The *Miranda* v. *Arizona* ruling was announced on June 13, 1966, three years and three months after Ernesto Miranda was arrested and three months and two weeks after the oral arguments were heard in the U.S. Supreme Court.

CITING PreceDenT

As we know, the justices laid down a solid foundation of precedent for their ruling in *Miranda*. Early in the opinion, Chief Justice Warren wrote: "We start here . . . with the premise that our [ruling] is not an innovation in our [laws], but is an application of principles long recognized and applied in other settings."

Among the cases cited as precedent were *Brown* v. *Mississippi* (1936), *Gideon* v. *Wainwright* (1963), *Malloy* v. *Hogan* (1964), and *Escobedo* v. *Illinois* (1964). The majority justices saw these cases as events moving the law in the direction of expanding suspects' Fifth and Sixth Amendment rights. So, according to these justices, their ruling here was part of a longstanding trend in U.S. federal law.

Still, the *Miranda* ruling was doing something new. It was setting down strict rules that law enforcement officers had to follow from the moment of arrest onward—rules that if not followed carefully could make suspects' confessions invalid. This was especially true when it came to the interrogation stage.

THE InTerroGaTIOn ISSue

Justice Warren's opinion about the type of interrogation methods used by the Chicago police in *Escobedo* and Fifth Amendment rights was that, "The current practice of [secret] interrogation is at odds with one of our Nation's most cherished principles—that the individual may not be compelled to incriminate himself. Unless adequate protective devices are employed . . . no statement obtained from the defendant can truly be the product of his free choice."

These "adequate protective devices" would be revealed later on. But first, the ruling reviewed the interrogation methods used by police in the four cases rolled into the *Miranda* ruling: "In the [four] cases before us today . . . we concern ourselves primarily with this interrogation atmosphere and the evils it can bring."

The ruling made special note of the *Westover* and *Stewart* cases.

> In *Westover* v. *United States* . . . the defendant was handed over to the Federal Bureau of Investigation by local authorities after they had detained and interrogated him for a lengthy period, both at night and the following morning. After some two hours of questioning, the federal officers had obtained signed statements from the defendant. . . . [I]n *California* v. *Stewart*, the local police held the defendant five days in the station and interrogated him on nine separate occasions before they secured his [incriminating] statement.

The ruling went on to say:

> To be sure, the records do not [show] overt physical coercion or [obvious] psychological ploys. The fact remains that in none of these cases did the officers undertake to afford appropriate safeguards at the outset of the interrogation to

insure that the statements were truly the product of free choice.

In other words, none of the suspects in these cases had made a voluntary confession. And in each case the police were to blame. "From the foregoing, we can readily perceive an intimate connection between the [Fifth Amendment] privilege against self-incrimination and police custodial questioning."

What should the police have done to insure that the suspects' confessions were voluntary? "At the outset, if a person in custody is to be subjected to interrogation, he must first be informed in clear and unequivocal terms that he has the right to remain silent." The ruling went on to say:

> [I]t is clear that Miranda was not in any way [made aware] of his right to consult with an attorney and to have one present during the interrogation, nor was his right not to be compelled to incriminate himself effectively protected in any other manner. Without these warnings the statements were inadmissible.

Which meant that Miranda's confession could not be used as evidence against him, which meant that the lower court verdict of guilty was overturned. Would he be re-tried for robbery and rape? That was up to the state of Arizona.

THE *MIRANDA* RIGHTS EXPLAINED

The ruling did not end there, though. Far more was at stake than Miranda's fate. The words that followed would affect countless police officers and criminal suspects in the years to come, not just in Arizona but nationwide:

[The defendant] must be warned prior to any questioning that he has the right to remain silent, that anything he says can be used against him in a court of law, that he has the right to the presence of an attorney, and that if he cannot afford an attorney one will be appointed to him prior to any questioning if he so desires. Opportunity to exercise these rights must be afforded to him throughout the interrogation.

The ruling explained these rights one by one. First, the right to remain silent: "At the outset, if a person in custody is to be subjected to interrogation, he must first be informed in clear and unequivocal terms that he has the right to remain silent." Why? Because "such a warning is an absolute prerequisite in overcoming the inherent pressures of the interrogation atmosphere." And "the warning will show the individual that his inter-rogators are prepared to recognize his privilege should he choose to exercise it."

Next, the Court explained the phrase "anything he says can be used against him in a court of law" this way:

This warning is needed in order to make [the sus-pect] aware not only of the privilege, but also of the consequences of forgoing it. . . . Moreover, this warning may serve to make the individual more acutely aware that he is . . . not in the pres-ence of persons acting solely in his interest.

Next came the right to an attorney. Notice how the Court responds to Nelson's argument that Miranda did not need a warning because he probably knew his rights already.

[The suspect] must be clearly informed that he has the right to consult with a lawyer and to have the lawyer with him during interrogation. . . . [T]his warning is an absolute prerequisite to interrogation. No amount of circumstantial evidence that the person may have been aware of this right will suffice to stand in its stead: Only through such a warning is there [proof] that the accused was aware of this right.

The ruling gives other important reasons for this right:

With a lawyer present the likelihood that the police will practice coercion is reduced, and if coercion is nevertheless exercised the lawyer can testify to it in court. The presence of a lawyer can also help to guarantee that the accused gives a fully accurate statement to the police and that the statement is rightly reported by the prosecution at trial.

Finally, the Court explained why this right must also apply to poor suspects.

The financial ability of the individual has no relationship to the scope of the rights involved here. The privilege against self-incrimination secured by the Constitution applies to all individuals. The need for counsel in order to protect the privilege exists for the poor as well as the affluent.

new sTanDarDs For voLunTary conFessIons

Rights have limits, and the Court took care to establish limits to the *Miranda* rights, based on custody and inter-

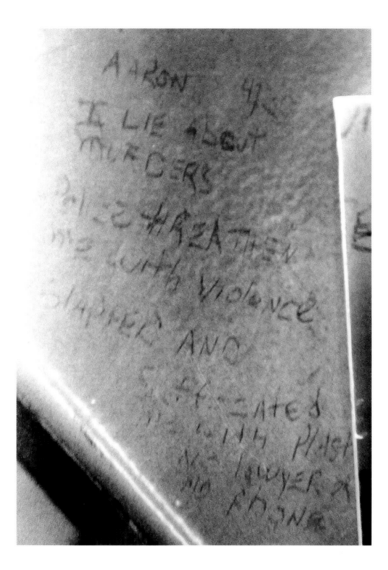

A METAL BENCH ON WHICH AARON PATTERSON CRUDELY SCRATCHED A MES-
SAGE DURING POLICE INTERROGATION ABOUT A DOUBLE MURDER IN CHICAGO.
"POLICE THREATEN ME WITH VIOLENCE. SLAPPED AND SUFFOCATED ME WITH
PLASTIC. NO LAWYER OR DAD. NO PHONE . . . SIGNED FALSE STATEMENT TO
MURDERS . . . AARON." THE *MIRANDA* DECISION, WHICH MEANT THAT A
LAWYER WOULD BE PRESENT DURING INTERROGATIONS, REDUCED THE LIKELI-
HOOD OF COERCION.

rogation. Police were required to read suspects their *Miranda* rights only after taking them into custody and before interrogating them.

Otherwise, police officers did not have to Mirandize people. They could ask anyone routine questions, such as name, address, and date of birth, to establish that person's identity. They could even give people alcohol and drug tests without issuing warnings. They could question people at a crime scene without first reading them their rights, as long they weren't indicted or under arrest. If those people made incriminating statements, those statements could be used against them later in court.

But once police took a suspect into custody, they had to read that person his or her rights before beginning interrogation. And if they did not read an arrested suspect his rights? Then there was a good chance that any incriminating statements would be declared involuntary and excluded from evidence.

Before the *Miranda* ruling, confessions were considered voluntary if they met the totality-of-circumstances standards. After *Miranda*, confessions still had to meet these standards, which individual states still set on their own, without federal interference. But now confessions also had to meet the *Miranda* standards. And it was now the individual state's responsibility to make sure that all suspects who needed a lawyer had one.

THE FAIRNESS ISSUE

The Court took care to make it clear that their ruling did not mean a suspect absolutely *had* to have an attorney during interrogation.

> There is no requirement that police stop a person who enters a police station and states that he

wishes to confess to a crime . . . or a person who
calls the police to offer a confession or any other
statement he desires to make. Volunteered statements of any kind are not barred by the Fifth
Amendment and their admissibility is not
affected by our holding today.

Police must inform suspects of their right to counsel,
and suspects are free to refuse that right. "After such
warnings have been given, and such opportunity afforded
him, the individual may knowingly and intelligently waive
these rights and agree to answer questions or make a
statement," the ruling stated. "But police must provide
proof of the suspect's refusal. Unless and until such warnings and waiver are demonstrated by the prosecution at
the trial, no evidence obtained as a result of the interrogation can be used against him."

The Court also made sure to say that its ruling was fair
to law enforcement. "Our decision is not intended to
hamper the traditional function of police officers in
investigating crime. . . . Confessions remain a proper ele-
ment in law enforcement." Police could still use pressure
to persuade a suspect to confess, but not coercion.
Physical force was still strictly forbidden, and so were out-
right lies and other forms of trickery in an interrogation
session.

Finally, the ruling acknowledged that *Miranda* v.
Arizona would mean that from now on criminal suspects
could expect to be treated fairly.

Today, then, there can be no doubt that the Fifth
Amendment privilege is available outside of criminal court proceedings [starting with arrest] and
serves to protect persons in all settings in which

their freedom of action is curtailed in any significant way from being compelled to incriminate themselves.

DISSENT

The dissent among the minority justices was vigorous. Justice John Marshall Harlan wrote a dissenting opinion in which he was joined by Justices Byron R. White and Potter Stewart. Harlan's strongly worded dissent began, "I believe the decision of the Court represents poor constitutional law and entails harmful consequences for the country at large." It went on to say:

> There can be little doubt that the Court's new code would markedly decrease the number of confessions. . . . How much harm this decision will inflict on law enforcement cannot fairly be predicted with accuracy. . . . We do know that some crimes cannot be solved without confessions . . . and that the Court is taking a real risk with society's welfare in imposing its new regime on the country. The social costs of crime are too great to call the new rules anything but a hazardous experimentation.

Harlan also focused on the issue of guarding against police coercion:

> The new rules are not designed to guard against police brutality or other unmistakably banned forms of coercion. Those who use third degree tactics and deny them in court are equally able and destined to lie as skillfully about warnings and waivers. Rather, the thrust of the new rules is to

negate all pressures, to reinforce the nervous or ignorant suspect, and ultimately to discourage any confession at all.

Harlan looked at the majority ruling from the viewpoint of a strict constructionist and found that it lacked grounding in the U.S. Constitution:

The Court's opinion in my view reveals no adequate basis for extending the Fifth Amendment's privilege against self-incrimination to the police station. . . . [T]he Fifth Amendment [prohibits] only compelling any person "in any criminal case to be a witness against himself."

In other words, "criminal case" means a courtroom, not a police station. Justice Harlan then expressed his outrage at the Court making a ruling that had freed a confessed rapist:

Miranda's oral and written confessions are now held inadmissible under the Court's new rules. One is entitled to feel astonished that the Constitution can be read to produce this result. These confessions were obtained during brief, daytime questioning conducted by two officers and unmarked by any of the traditional [signs] of coercion. They assured a conviction for a brutal and unsettling crime, for which the police had and quite possibly could obtain little evidence other than the victim's identifications, evidence which is frequently unreliable.

Harlan was referring to a well-known fact in criminal law cases: Identifications of suspects by eyewitnesses

NOT-SO-reliaBLE EYEWITNESSES

Think about it: you catch a glimpse of a criminal fleeing the scene of a crime. Later on you must look at a lineup in which four strangers who all look somewhat alike stand facing you. If one is the person you saw fleeing the crime scene, what are your chances of picking him out of the lineup?

Research studies, in general, show that your chances are not much better than 50 percent. Nearly as often as not, you are likely to pick the wrong person. Pressure is one big reason. You saw this person in a scary situation, and now you're under pressure to identify him. But even without the stress, studies show that people are simply not very good at identifying strangers they have seen only briefly.

Juries still tend to believe eyewitness testimony. But then, most jurors do not know about these research studies. That's why defense attorneys call the experts who conduct these studies to testify about how unreliable eyewitness identifications can be.

RESEARCH HAS SHOWN THAT THE CHANCES OF CHOOSING THE CORRECT ASSAILANT FROM A POLICE LINEUP IS NO MORE THAN FIFTY-FIFTY.

often turn out to be mistaken. With only eyewitness testimony and without a confession, a guilty suspect stands a
good chance of being found not guilty.

In an interview years later, John P. Frank admitted
that his client probably did commit crimes. But, he
said, they may not have been as serious as the crimes
he ended up confessing to in Interrogation Room #2
without an attorney to advise him of his rights.

But even if Miranda was guilty as charged, the outcome was justified, Frank believed. Even if it did overturn
a guilty verdict for a guilty suspect, *Miranda* would help
many more suspects in the years to come, to make sure
that the innocent did not end up in prison.

ASSOCIATE JUSTICE TOM CLARK WROTE A DISSENT IN WHICH HE ARGUED THAT MAKING POLICE GIVE WARNINGS BEFORE INTERROGATIONS MIGHT STOP CRIMINALS FROM MAKING CONFESSIONS.

seven
REACTIONS TO THE RULING

JUSTICE TOM C. CLARK also wrote a dissent to the *Miranda* majority opinion. In it, he stated that the warnings "inserted at the nerve center of crime detection may well kill the patient." That is, making the police give the warnings before interrogation may mean that criminals will stop confessing entirely.

Clark's reasoning went something like this: You have a suspect who is about to admit that he did something criminal—something that will send him to jail. Wait, you tell him. Before you say another word, listen to what I, the arresting officer—the person in charge, have to tell you.

Then you warn the suspect about what could happen to him unless he changes his mind—that his confession could put him behind bars. Now what can we reasonably expect the suspect to do next? Wouldn't that warning make him stop and ask himself, "Hold on, what am I about to do here? This makes no sense. All I'd be doing is dooming myself to a stretch behind bars. Oh no, I'm not saying anything until I talk to that lawyer you say you'll supply me."

A HEATED ATMOSPHERE
The 1966 *Miranda* ruling came at a time when crime in the streets was a deadly serious issue. Each year the FBI

miranda cards

The Court's ruling did not set down the exact words that police must use when giving suspects *Miranda* warnings. It was up to individual police departments to come up with their own wording. So departments had wallet-sized cards printed up for each officer to carry. A typical card includes statements such as these:

> · You have the right to remain silent.
> ·Anything you say can and will be used against you in a court of law.
> ·You have the right to talk to a lawyer and have him present with you during questioning.
> ·If you cannot afford a lawyer, one will be appointed to represent you.
> ·Do you understand each of these rights as I have explained them to you?
> ·Having these rights in mind, do you wish to talk to us now?

WARNING AS TO YOUR RIGHTS

You are under arrest. Before we ask you any questions, you must understand what your rights are.

You have the right to remain silent. You are not required to say anything to us at any time or to answer any questions. Anything you say can be used against you in court.

You have the right to talk to a lawyer for advice before we question you and to have him with you during questioning.

If you cannot afford a lawyer and want one, a lawyer will be provided for you.

If you want to answer questions now without a lawyer present you will still have the right to stop answering at any time. You also have the right to stop answering at any time until you talk to a lawyer.   P-4475

AFTER THE MIRANDA DECISION, MANY POLICE DEPARTMENTS MADE UP WALLET-SIZED CARDS SIMILAR TO THIS ONE SO THAT POLICE OFFICERS WOULD NOT HAVE TO THINK UP WHAT WORDS TO USE TO GIVE THE WARNING EACH TIME THEY ARRESTED A SUSPECT.

publishes national crime statistics. Since 1957 the rate of crimes in the United States had been generally on the rise, and that included violent crimes. Two years before *Miranda*, Republican presidential candidate Barry Goldwater said, "Crime grows faster than population, while those who break the law are accorded more consideration than those who try to enforce the law. . . . Law breakers are defended. Our wives, all women, feel unsafe in our streets."

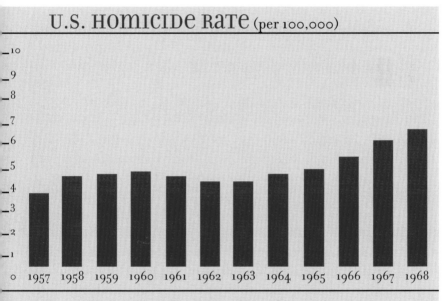

U.S. HOMICIDE RATE (per 100,000)

Source: *Crime in the United States, FBI Uniform Crime Reports,* 2002

In this heated atmosphere, some people reacted to *Miranda* with alarm, especially some law enforcement officers. They saw the ruling as a sharp personal reprimand with unfair penalties attached. The nation's highest court had openly criticized their working methods. It had also saddled them with restrictions that protected the rights of criminals at the expense of the public's right to be safe and secure. Some police officers also believed the ruling would encourage criminals to commit more crimes, since authorities would now have a tougher time bringing them to justice.

And the criticism escalated. In 1968, two years after *Miranda*, Richard Nixon was the Republican candidate for president. In a campaign speech, Nixon said, "[T]he cumulative impact of these decisions [*Escobedo* and *Miranda*] has been to set free . . . guilty individuals on the basis of legal technicalities. The tragic lesson of guilty men walking free from hundreds of courtrooms around the country has not been lost on the criminal community."

conGress reacTs

Congress also reacted. Lawmakers could not change the *Miranda* ruling itself. Only the U.S. Supreme Court could do that. But they could water it down, and one passage in the *Miranda* ruling gave lawmakers the chance to do this:

> Congress and the States are free to develop their own safeguards for the privilege [against self-incrimination], so long as they are fully as effective as [the Miranda warnings] in informing accused persons of their right of silence and in affording a continuous opportunity to exercise it.

So Congress passed statutory law 3501, which stated that the *Miranda* warnings were not the only factor that a federal judge may use to decide whether a confession was voluntary. Statutory law 3501 was part of the Omnibus Crime Control and Safe Streets Act of 1968. The new law first mentioned all the factors that went into the traditional "totality-of-circumstances" approach. Then it added the *Miranda* warnings as one more factor. "The presence or absence of any of the above-mentioned factors to be taken into consideration by the judge need not be conclusive on the issue of voluntariness of the confession," the new law said.

In other words, the *Miranda* warnings were not absolutely necessary. A federal judge could still find a suspect's confession voluntary even if the police or federal agents had never issued them.

The new law was not welcomed in federal courts, however. Clearly, 3501 was in direct conflict with the *Miranda* ruling. To rely on it in a trial court would almost certainly mean losing the case on appeal. So federal authorities ignored 3501—for the time being. Statutory law 3501 would be challenged in the U.S. Supreme Court in 2000.

GOOD NEWS

Six months after *Miranda* went into effect, one thing was becoming clear: the extremely negative reactions were just that—extreme. People came to realize that the *Miranda* warnings were not as new or as revolutionary as they had once thought. After all, the FBI had been issuing them since the 1940s. Really, the warnings were only new at the state level. And they were not having the negative effects on state law enforcement that people had imagined.

Justice Tom C. Clark had predicted that *Miranda* would stop criminals from confessing. But after talking with police officials across the country, he had changed his mind. In fact, he said, the opposite was true. More people were confessing since *Miranda*, not fewer.

And the more time that passed, the more *Miranda* was accepted. In 1976, U.S. Attorney General Griffin Bell said that the law enforcement community now saw the *Miranda* warnings as a necessary part of their job.8 In 1986, Mario Merola, a Bronx County, New York, district attorney, said that *Miranda* hadn't harmed law enforcement at all. In fact, authorities in his county were successfully prosecuting more criminals than ever.

Statistical studies showed that *Miranda* had not led to the predicted flood of excluded confessions. A July 1988 *Newsweek* magazine article reported that fewer than one percent of criminal cases had been dismissed due to excluded confessions. And of this one percent, only a small fraction were dismissed because police failed to issue proper *Miranda* warnings.

And what of the fears about rising costs? People had predicted that *Miranda* would cost taxpayers huge amounts of money, since states would have to hire thousands of new public defenders for poor suspects. But these fears had not come true either. The overwhelming majority of suspects continued to waive their right to an attorney during interrogation, and their confessions still held up in court.

As more time passed, people saw that *Miranda* actually saved the courts money as well as time and trouble. In a 1984 opinion, Supreme Court Justice Thurgood Marshall wrote that before *Miranda* the lower courts "found it exceedingly difficult to determine whether a given confession had been coerced. . . . Courts around the country were spending countless hours reviewing the facts of individual custodial interrogations."

Why? Because courts had no clear, uniform standard for judging whether a confession was voluntary and not coerced. *Miranda* gave them that standard.

eight
EXCEPTIONS AND EXTENSIONS

LIKE OTHER CONTROVERSIAL Court rulings, *Miranda* would draw wave after wave of challenge and change in years to come. It was natural. One Court ruling put it this way:

> No court laying down a general rule can possibly foresee the various circumstances in which counsel will seek to apply it, and the sort of modifications represented by these cases are as much a normal part of constitutional law as the original decision.

As police officers, lawyers, and judges apply the ruling in new and different situations, they raise challenging questions. And the answers to those questions mean change.

For example, police had to read a person his *Miranda* rights when they arrested him. But exactly when was a person under arrest? The ruling also stated that the suspect could waive his *Miranda* rights and confess. But police must prove that the suspect had waived his rights, and what constituted valid proof that would stand up in court?

Since these questions were not answered in the ruling itself, they would have to be answered in rulings to come. The Court treated *Miranda* as it had treated *Escobedo*, with wary anticipation. The justices kept an eye out for certs that focused on *Miranda*-related questions.

Some of these questions would lead the Court to make exceptions to *Miranda* that would narrow and weaken the ruling. Others would lead them to extend the ruling, widening and strengthening it. Let's look first at the exceptions.

EXCEPTIONS: IMPEACHING WITNESSES

A major exception to *Miranda* came with the Court's ruling in *Harris* v. *New York* (1971). The question focused on impeaching witnesses. *Impeach* has two different meanings. To impeach a president or a Supreme Court justice is to remove him or her from office for misconduct. To impeach a witness is to destroy the witness's credibility, to make him or her out to be a liar.

Here are the facts in the case. The defendant, a man named Vivien Harris, was charged with selling heroin to undercover police officers. After his arrest, Harris made statements to police that amounted to a confession.

But the trial court judge ruled that Harris's incriminating statements could not be used as evidence against him. Why not? Because when they took him into custody, police had not warned the suspect of his Sixth Amendment right to counsel. At the trial, police detectives testified that Harris had confessed. But Harris insisted that he had not, and that made it a deadlock: the detectives' word against the defendant's.

To break the deadlock, the prosecutor used a surprise tactic. He read Harris's suppressed confession to the jury—but not as a confession. That was not allowed. Instead, the prosecutor read it to show the jury that Harris had changed his story. On the stand he said he was innocent, yet earlier he said he was guilty, as the suppressed confession clearly showed. As a result, Harris was convicted, and the New York State Supreme Court let the conviction stand.

The question before the U.S. Supreme Court in *Harris* was this: Could a confession that was excluded because it violated the *Miranda* ruling be used to impeach a defendant's credibility—to make him out a liar to the jury?

The Court that heard the *Harris* argument in 1971 was not the Court that heard *Miranda* in 1966. Earl Warren had retired. The new Chief Justice was Warren Burger, appointed by President Richard Nixon in 1969. And Abe Fortas had been replaced by Harry A. Blackmun. Both Burger and Blackmun were closer to being strict constructionists than the activists they had replaced. The Burger Court ruled 5 to 4 in favor of the state of New York. *Harris* created an exception to *Miranda*. Now an excluded confession could be used to impeach a witness.

EXCEPTIONS: PUBLIC SAFETY

Another major exception to *Miranda* came with the 1984 ruling in *New York* v. *Quarles*. The ruling focused on this question: When police officers capture a suspect they believe has hidden a dangerous weapon in a public place, must they read him his *Miranda* rights before asking him where the weapon is?

Here are the facts in the case. A police officer searching for a suspect in a grocery store spotted a man who matched the suspect's description. The suspect, Benjamin Quarles, ran, but the officer caught him at the back of the store. When he frisked Quarles, the officer found an empty shoulder holster.

Where was the gun? he asked. The suspect told him, and the officer retrieved the weapon, a .38 caliber revolver, from an empty carton on a store shelf. Only then did he read the suspect his *Miranda* rights.

Because the rights were read after the gun was found and not before, the trial court judge would not allow the suspect's statement about the hidden gun to be used against him. The judge also excluded the gun itself from evidence.

The state of New York appealed these exclusions. The officer's concern for public safety should come before the need to give warnings, the state's attorney argued. After all, a customer or an accomplice of the suspect might have got hold of the gun. But state appeals courts agreed with the trial judge. So the state took its appeal to the U.S. Supreme Court.

The Court agreed with the state and reversed the lower court exclusions with these words: "We conclude that under the circumstances involved in this case, overriding considerations of public safety justify the officer's failure to provide *Miranda* warnings before he asked questions devoted to locating the abandoned weapon."

The Court's decision was clear. When public safety was at issue, exceptions to *Miranda* could be made.

EXCEPTIONS: THE UNDERCOVER AGENT

This case, *Illinois* v. *Perkins* (1990), is known as the undercover exception to *Miranda*. A prisoner boasted to his cellmate that he had committed murder. The prisoner, Lloyd Perkins, was serving time for another offense.

Perkins' cellmate, Donald Charlton, told the authorities about Perkins' confession. Police responded by placing an undercover agent, Parisi, in the cell with Charlton and Perkins. Only Charlton knew Parisi's true identity. Perkins thought Parisi was just another cellmate. Here is some of a secretly recorded conversation between Perkins and Agent Parisi:

> Parisi: You ever do [murder] anyone?
> Perkins: Yeah, once in East St. Louis, [Illinois] in a rich white neighborhood. . . .
> Parisi: How long ago did this happen?
> Perkins: Approximately about two years ago. I got paid $5,000 for that job.
> Parisi: How did it go down?
> Perkins: I walked up [to] this guy['s] house with a sawed-off [shotgun] under my trench coat.

Naturally, Parisi did not Mirandize Perkins before talking with him. That would have blown his cover. Parisi's undercover work succeeded in getting Perkins brought to trial for murder. But the trial judge excluded their conversation from evidence on grounds of *Miranda* violations.

The state of Illinois appealed the exclusion but lost. The state appeals court ruled that *Miranda* prohibited undercover contacts with prisoners if they might produce incriminating statements from the prisoner.

The U.S. Supreme Court disagreed and reversed the lower court decisions to exclude. From then on undercover conversations could be included as evidence even though no *Miranda* warnings were given. Here is the Court's reasoning behind the reversal:

> It is *Miranda*'s premise that the danger of coercion results from the interaction of custody and official interrogation. . . . That coercive atmosphere is not present when [a prisoner]

speaks freely to someone whom he believes to be a fellow inmate.

But the Court also made it clear in the *Perkins* ruling that *Miranda* did not stop police from putting pressure on a suspect to confess: "Ploys to mislead a suspect or lull him into a false sense of security that do not rise to the level of compulsion or coercion to speak are not within *Miranda*'s concerns."

EXTENSIONS: THE RIGHT TO an ATTorney

Now let's look at rulings that broadened and strengthened *Miranda*. First, we should recall that *Powell* v. *Alabama* (1932) and *Gideon* v. *Wainwright* (1963) both extended the right of counsel to poor defendants, and that *Miranda* further extended it to felony suspects at the interrogation stage.

Felonies are crimes punishable by a year or more in jail. Misdemeanors are less serious crimes, punishable by less than a year. After *Miranda*, some states extended the right of counsel to poor defendants charged with misdemeanors. Others did not. With its ruling in *Argersinger* v. *Hamlin* (1972), the Court set up one uniform law in regard to right of counsel for defendants charged with misdemeanors at the state level.

Here are the facts in the case. The petitioner, Argersinger, was charged with the misdemeanor crime of carrying a concealed weapon. In Florida, where the crime occurred, this offense could bring six months in jail. Argersinger was poor and not represented by counsel at his trial. He was found guilty and sentenced to ninety days.

Argersinger petitioned the Florida State Supreme Court. He asked the court to overturn his conviction because he had been deprived of his Sixth Amendment right to counsel. But Argersinger lost. The state appeals court upheld the trial court verdict. In Florida, a defendant was entitled to counsel only if the offense was punishable by more than six months in jail, the court said.

In its *Argersinger* ruling, the U.S. Supreme Court unanimously overturned the lower court decisions. The ruling stated, "No accused may be deprived of his liberty as the result of any criminal prosecution, whether felony or misdemeanor, in which he was denied the assistance of counsel."

EXTENSIONS: THE RIGHT TO REMAIN SILENT

Two important *Miranda*-related rulings widened the scope of the right to remain silent. The first was *Edwards* v. *Arizona* (1981). The petitioner, Edwards, was arrested for robbery. After being read his rights he agreed to answer questions, but then changed his mind and asked for an attorney. The police stopped the questioning and took Edwards to the county jail.

The next morning two detectives came to see him. Edwards said he did not want to talk to them without a lawyer, but they insisted. He had to talk, the detectives said. After again reading Edwards his *Miranda* rights, they managed to get him to confess. Edwards was tried and convicted, largely because of this confession. The Arizona State Supreme Court agreed, ruling that his confession was voluntary.

But in its *Edwards* ruling, the U.S. Supreme Court disagreed. The Court ruled that once a suspect has asked for counsel, he cannot be questioned further until counsel is provided "unless the accused has himself initiated further communication . . . with the police," which Edwards clearly had not.

The Court again widened the scope of the right to remain silent in its *Minnick* v. *Mississippi* (1990) ruling. Petitioner Minnick was arrested on a federal warrant for capital murder. Federal law enforcement officials questioned him, but stopped when he asked for counsel. A lawyer was appointed for Minnick, and they talked together.

Later, a county deputy sheriff insisted that Minnick talk with him. When Minnick tried to refuse, the deputy said that he couldn't, that Minnick had to talk. After further questioning, which did not include any physical abuse, Minnick confessed to the murder.

Minnick's motion to suppress the confession was denied, and he was convicted and sentenced to death. The Mississippi State Supreme Court turned down Minnick's appeal. After all, the court reasoned, Minnick had been provided with counsel before he confessed, even though counsel was not present when he actually did confess.

The U.S. Supreme Court ruled in Minnick's favor by a vote of 6 to 3. In its ruling, the Court stated that "The issue in the case before us is whether [the protection granted in *Edwards*] ceases once the suspect has consulted with an attorney." The Court ruled that this protection does not end "unless the accused himself initiates further communication . . . with the police," which Minnick clearly had not.

DISSENT

One of the minority in *Minnick*, Justice Antonin Scalia, crafted a strongly worded dissent. He wrote that after a suspect has seen an attorney, as Minnick had, he almost certainly knows of his right to remain silent. And so Minnick's confession should be seen as honest, voluntary, and perfectly admissible as evidence. Scalia goes on to say:

> [I]t is wrong . . . to regard an honest confession as a "mistake." . . . A confession is rightly regarded by the sentencing guidelines as warranting a reduction of sentence, because it [shows personal responsibility for criminal conduct], which is the beginning of reform. We should, then, rejoice at an honest confession, rather than pity the "poor fool" who has made it.

Whether or not we agree with Justice Scalia, his views take us back to the 1930s, to the days of *Brown* v. *Mississippi* and *Powell* v. *Alabama*, when poor suspects could be beaten until they confessed and denied counsel at trial. We can't help but notice how much law enforcement practices have changed from the days when abusing suspects, physically and mentally, was seen as a routine practice.

ASSOCIATE JUSTICE ANTONIN SCALIA HAS DISSENTED TO EXTENSIONS OF *MIRANDA* RIGHTS IN CASES BROUGHT BEFORE TODAY'S COURT.

nine
MIRANDA IS CHALLENGED

IN THE YEAR 2000 the Court took up the most serious challenge yet to *Miranda*, a head-on attempt to overturn it. *Dickerson* v. *United States* (2000) was based on Statutory law 3501, passed by Congress in 1968 for that very purpose. Law 3501 told federal authorities that some confessions could be used as evidence in court even if police did not give the suspect *Miranda* warnings. Federal authorities had elected not to enforce 3501 because they thought it was unconstitutional.

But was it? The Court took up *Dickerson* to settle the question once and for all.

The petitioner, Charles Dickerson, was tried in federal court, in Alexandria, Virginia, for eighteen bank robberies across three states. Dickerson had confessed during interrogation without being read his *Miranda* rights. That was why the federal judge in the case excluded the confession from evidence.

The U.S. government appealed the exclusion, and a U.S. District Court of appeals ruled in the government's favor, based on statutory law 3501. As we know, this federal law made the giving of *Miranda* warnings only one factor among several in deciding whether a confession was voluntary. The District Court said that even though Dickerson had not received *Miranda* warnings, his confession could be included in evidence.

So Dickerson appealed to the U.S. Supreme Court. The Court identified the question it faced in *Dickerson* this way:

> Because of the obvious conflict between our decision in *Miranda* and 3501, we must address whether Congress has constitutional authority to thus [overrule] *Miranda*. If Congress has such authority, 3501's totality-of-the-circumstances approach must prevail over *Miranda*'s requirement of warnings; if not, [3501] must yield to *Miranda*'s more specific requirements.

THe Government's POSITION

Dickerson proved to be a most unusual case. The respondent, the U.S. government, represented by the Department of Justice (DOJ), agreed with Dickerson, the petitioner. DOJ did not want to see statutory law 3501 overrule *Miranda*. "At this point in time, thirty-three years after *Miranda* was decided and many years after it has been absorbed into police practices, judicial procedures and the public understanding, the *Miranda* decision should not be overruled," the DOJ brief said.

Many members of the law enforcement community felt that *Miranda* provided much-needed guidelines for police officers nationwide. If *Miranda* warnings were not required, then police could no longer be sure how to guarantee that suspects' constitutional rights were properly upheld.

PAUL CASSELL ARGUED FOR THE U.S. GOVERNMENT IN THE CASE OF *DICKERSON* V. *UNITED STATES* (2000). THE GOVERNMENT SOUGHT TO OVERTURN THE *MIRANDA* DECISION, BUT DID NOT SUCCEED.

THE RESPONDENT'S POSITION

Someone had to argue the case for the respondent, the U.S. government, so the government called in a highly respected law professor. Paul Cassell of the University of Utah was a longtime *Miranda* opponent. Cassell wrote a brief opposing the *Miranda* law. In it, he hit on these key points:

- *Miranda* is an extreme remedy for dealing with police abuse of suspects' rights. It automatically excludes confessions, while 3501 deals with the problem in a far more reasonable manner, bringing several factors into the decision-making process.

• The Court went beyond its authority when it made the *Miranda* ruling. Instead of interpreting laws, which is the Court's proper function, it became the maker of laws, bypassing the lawmakers in Congress.

• The exceptions that have been made to *Miranda* through the years show it to be a weak law that does not appear to be constitutional.

• *Miranda* has made law enforcement a tougher task. Instead of actively bringing suspects to justice, police must help them in deciding whether and when to talk to them about their crimes. Rather than search for the truth, police must now play by rules that actually help a suspect conceal the truth. This can only undermine the public's confidence in the criminal justice system.

Seventy-five percent of FBIAA (FBI Agents Association) members are FBI agents. The organization filed an amicus curiae brief in support of the respondent, the U.S. government, which stated: "No one disputes that Dickerson's confession was voluntary, and not the result of any coercion. The only issue in dispute was the technical issue of whether he was read his *Miranda* warnings before or after the confession."

The FBIAA brief voiced a common complaint about *Miranda*: Because of the ruling, guilty people were being let off on technical points that had nothing to do with their guilt or innocence.

THE RULING
The Court ruled 7 to 2 in favor of the petitioner, Dickerson, and against statutory law 3501. *Miranda* was not only

allowed to stand, it was strengthened. The majority opinion in *Dickerson* stated: "We . . . hold that *Miranda* and [the cases after it] govern the admissibility of statements made during custodial interrogation in both state and federal courts." In other words, *Miranda* now applied equally in all U.S. courts at all levels. There were no exceptions.

The ruling went on to show that *Dickerson* had been a battle between two of the three branches of government, the legislative and the judicial: "In sum, we conclude that *Miranda* announced a constitutional rule that Congress may not supersede legislatively." That is, the Court declared statutory law 3501 unconstitutional. The judicial branch had won the battle.

However, the Court did not ignore the criticisms voiced by *Miranda* opponents. Could it lead to guilty suspects going free? "The disadvantage of the *Miranda* rule is that statements which may be [voluntary], made by a defendant who is aware of his 'rights,' may nonetheless be excluded and a guilty defendant go free as a result," the Court admitted.

Did that mean that 3501 was the better path to take? The Court answered this way: "But experience suggests that the totality-of-the-circumstances test which 3501 seeks to revive is more difficult than *Miranda* for law enforcement officers to conform to, and for courts to apply in a consistent manner. . . ."

By now the Court had fewer activist judges than strict constructionists. It was a more conservative court than the Warren Court. Yet it still upheld the *Miranda* ruling, despite opposition from the law enforcement community. This quote from the Justice Department's *Dickerson* brief may best sum up why it did so: "In our view *Miranda* has come to play a unique and important role in the nation's conception of our criminal justice system: it promotes public confidence that the criminal justice system is fair."

DISSenT

As he did in *Minnick*, Scalia dissented strongly from the *Dickerson* decision. Justice Scalia was known as the Court's strictest constructionist and most outspoken critic of the majority ruling in *Miranda* v. *Arizona*. He used his *Dickerson* dissent to declare, in no uncertain terms, what he thought of *Miranda*.

When the Court handed down *Miranda*, Scalia wrote, it was not properly interpreting the Constitution but improperly expanding it, "imposing what it regards as useful . . . restrictions upon Congress and the States. That is an immense and frightening anti-democratic power, and it does not exist."

What did Justice Scalia think about the *Miranda* right to counsel at the interrogation stage?

> There is a world of difference . . . between compelling a suspect to incriminate himself and preventing him from foolishly doing so of his own accord. . . . Counsel's presence is not required to tell the suspect that he *need* not speak; the interrogators can do that.

And Scalia wrote this about *Miranda*'s attitude toward confessions: "[W]hat is most remarkable about the *Miranda* decision . . . is its [obvious] hostility toward the act of confession *per se*, rather than toward what the Constitution abhors, *compelled* confession."

But for all his passion against *Miranda*, Justice Scalia was in the minority, not just of the Court but of the country as a whole. *Miranda* continues to be a well-accepted part of police procedure. But that hasn't kept it from continuing to be a flash point of controversy.

ten
MIRANDA TODAY

SOME PEOPLE breathed a huge sigh of relief when the Court ruled in Dickerson's favor. Among them was the editorial board of *The Nation*, a magazine known for its support of human rights. A *Nation* editorial said: "The court's ruling in *Dickerson* does not just insure that *Miranda*'s famous language will be enshrined in another generation of cop shows. . . . [I]t signals what appears to be a pendulum swing away from unbridled vengeance as the driving force of American criminal law."

After *Dickerson*, the *Miranda* rule would be widely seen as a legitimate Fifth Amendment right and not just a rule made by judges to protect suspects. But that would not stop it from being the target of one legal challenge after another. The editorial board of the national newspaper *USA Today* pointed this out in a 2003 editorial:

> Thirty-seven years after it was decided, the *Miranda* decision remains the Supreme Court's most contentious criminal procedure ruling. The court has revisited the ruling nearly 50 times, expanding and clarifying the right and establishing exceptions that allow police and prosecutors to use some confessions even if a proper warning wasn't given.

What is it about *Miranda* that makes it so contentious, so open to challenge and revision, even today, four decades after it was announced? Two factors are the primary targets of these challenges today: custody and interrogation. Both are especially open to interpretation and argument. Let's look at some recent *Miranda*-based U.S. Supreme Court rulings to see how *Miranda* is changing today. We'll begin with a case that focuses on the custody factor.

YARBOROUGH V. ALVARADO (2004)

Custody is not a simple matter. "In custody" is another way of saying "under arrest." Yet a suspect can be considered in legal custody even if the officer questioning him never tells him, "You are under arrest." Two situations together add up to legal custody. The suspect must believe that he or she is under suspicion of committing a crime, and the suspect must feel that he or she is in an unfamiliar, hostile place and is not free to leave. Then the officer must read the suspect the *Miranda* warnings before interrogation can begin.

On the other hand, suspects can walk into a police station of their own free will and confess to a crime and agree to answer any questions put to them by the officers and still not be in custody—as long as they feel free to leave any time they want. Under these circumstances, police can go ahead and question suspects without placing them under arrest and reading them their *Miranda* rights.

These circumstances were crucial in the case of Michael Alvarado. He was seventeen years old—still a minor—when he and a friend tried to steal a truck, which led to the shooting death of the truck's owner. Alvarado was a prime suspect when Los Angeles police called his home and asked him to come to the station for an interview with Officer Comstock.

At this point Alvarado was not under arrest or charged with any crime. He was just there to answer some questions. The questioning took place in a room with only the officer and the suspect present. It lasted about two hours, and no *Miranda* warnings were given.

At first, Alvarado flatly denied that he'd had anything to do with the situation, but little by little his story changed. Finally, he admitted that he and his friend did try to steal the victim's truck and then conceal the gun after the murder took place.

During the interview, Comstock asked Alvarado twice whether he would like take a break, and each time Alvarado declined. When it was over, Comstock returned Alvarado to his parents, who drove him home from the station.

CUSTODY and YOUTH

After Alvarado was charged with murder and attempted robbery, he asked the trial court judge to suppress the statements he'd made during questioning. He argued that he should have been read his *Miranda* warnings because he was in custody. The judge denied his motion, and Alvarado was found guilty of attempted robbery and second degree murder.

He appealed the decision to two state appeals courts but lost both times. They ruled that a *Miranda* warning was not necessary during questioning because the suspect was not in custody at the time.

But the third appeals court reversed the conviction. The panel of judges based the reversal on the fact that Alvarado was only seventeen. Being a minor, he was not experienced enough to realize that he was not in custody and could have left the room at any time. In other words, because of his youth, Alvarado had been coerced into making a confession.

The state of California appealed that ruling to the U.S. Supreme Court, which accepted the case. The state insisted that Alavarado had not been in custody and so was not coerced. Here is how the Court saw things:

> The police did not transport [Michael Alvarado] to the station or require him to appear at a particular time; . . . they did not threaten him or suggest he would be placed under arrest; . . . his parents remained in the lobby during the interview, suggesting that the interview would be brief; . . . Comstock twice asked Alvarado if he wanted to take a break; and, at the end of the interview, Alvarado went home.

Those facts suggested that Alvarado was not in custody. However, the Court added, other facts suggested that he might have been:

> Comstock did not tell Alvarado that he was free to leave; he was brought to the station by his legal guardians rather than arriving on his own accord; and his parents allegedly asked to be present at the interview but were [refused].

After weighing both sets of facts, the Court ruled 5 to 4 against Alvarado, upholding his trial court convictions for robbery and murder. The Court made it clear that the key to Alvarado's argument, that he was minor, did not figure in the ruling: "The Court's opinions applying the *Miranda* custody test have not mentioned the suspect's age, much less mandated its consideration."

That is, neither the 1966 *Miranda* ruling nor any of the *Miranda*-related rulings since had mentioned the suspect's age. As the Court saw it, Alvarado was not in custody during questioning, and so the police did not have to read him his *Miranda* rights.

WHAT IS INTERROGATION?

Now we'll look at cases that focus on the interrogation factor.

In legal terms, there are three distinctly different kinds of questioning. First, there is the normal, casual variety: "How are you feeling today? Is everything all right?" Then there is direct questioning: "What did you see when you drove by the house? Did you hear any unusual noises?" Finally, there is interrogation. This is questioning that carries the unmistakable message that you, the person being questioned, are a suspect in a crime: "Where were you between the hours of 11 PM and 1 AM? Do you own a .32 caliber handgun?"

Unlike the other forms of questioning, interrogation involves pressure and persuasion. It is questioning with a clear goal in mind: to get the suspect to confess to the crime, or at least to admit that he played some part in it. A good interrogator knows how to use words, tone of voice, gestures, and body movements to persuade a suspect to help convict himself.

Sometimes the pressure begins with soft, kind words and concerned smiles. "Are you comfortable? Anything I can get you?" The interrogator treats the suspect like a friend to get him off balance. Then, suddenly: "By the way, where were you on the night of April 21st?" Now the interrogation has begun.

As we learned from the Wickersham Report, police are

well-schooled in using different interrogation strategies, and some of them border on the illegal. Here is an example from a recent *Miranda*-related U.S. Supreme Court ruling.

FeLLers v. *unITeD STaTes* [2004]

The question in this case was: Exactly when are officers legally obligated to read *Miranda* rights to a suspect who is under indictment for a crime? Before they take him to the place where they will formally interrogate him, or after?

Police officers went to John Fellers' home in Lincoln, Nebraska, to question him about selling the illegal drug methamphetamine. They told him they had a warrant for his arrest, which meant that he was officially in custody.

But they did not immediately handcuff Fellers and take him in. Instead, they talked with him in his home for fifteen minutes or so. During that time, Fellers made several statements that implicated him in the crime.

After police took Fellers to jail, they read him his *Miranda* rights. He then signed a waiver saying he was voluntarily giving up those rights, and repeated the statements he had made at home, before police read him his rights.

Fellers later asked to have all his statements to police suppressed under the *Miranda* rule, and a hearing judge agreed. All statements would be suppressed because police had waited to read Fellers his *Miranda* rights until they took him to jail.

But the trial judge allowed the jury to hear the statements Fellers had made in jail, after he was read his rights and had waived them. As a result, Fellers was found guilty and sentenced to more than twelve years in federal prison.

The U.S. Supreme Court reversed the lower court conviction by a 9 to 0 vote. Citing a previous ruling, the Court wrote, "An accused is denied the protections of the Sixth

Amendment 'when there [are] used against him at his trial . . . his own incriminating words, which federal courts . . . deliberately elicited from him after he had been indicted and in the absence of counsel.'"

In its *Fellers* ruling, the Court also made a strong statement to police. They were not to try and get confessions from criminal suspects like Fellers, who were under indictment, without first telling them about their right to consult with a lawyer.

QUESTION FIRST

Finally, a *Miranda*-related case from 2004 hinged on whether a certain method of police interrogation was coercive. The respondent, Patrice Seibert, lived in a Rolla, Missouri, mobile home park. She had a twelve-year-old son, Jonathan, with cerebral palsy, a paralysis due to brain damage, which causes partial loss of muscle control.

One night Jonathan died in his sleep. Seibert feared that somehow she would be blamed for her son's death, that authorities might charge her with child neglect. So she asked two of her teenage sons and their friends for help. Together, they devised a plan to conceal the facts of Jonathan's death by burning the family's mobile home, and Jonathan's body with it.

As part of the plan, Seibert decided to leave a family friend in the mobile home with Jonathan's body. That way authorities could not accuse her of leaving him home alone. The family friend was Donald Rector, a mentally ill teenager. One of Seibert's sons and a friend started the fire, which destroyed the mobile home and burned Jonathan's body—and killed Rector in the process.

Five days later, police brought Patrice Seibert in for questioning. After Officer Richard Hanrahan questioned her for about forty minutes, Seibert admitted that Rector's death was no accident. He was meant to die in the fire, she confessed.

Seibert was then given a twenty-minute coffee break, after which Officer Hanrahan switched on a tape recorder and read Seibert the *Miranda* warnings. Seibert said she would waive her right to a lawyer and signed a paper confirming this. The officer then reminded her of the incriminating statements she had made before he read her the warnings.

> Hanrahan: Now, in discussion you told us . . . that there was a[n] understanding about Donald.
>
> Seibert: Yes.
>
> Hanrahan: Did that take place earlier that morning?
>
> Seibert: Yes.
>
> Hanrahan: And what was the understanding about Donald?
>
> Seibert: If they could get him out of the trailer, to take him out of the trailer.
>
> Hanrahan: And if they couldn't?
>
> Seibert: I, I never even thought about it. I just figured they would.
>
> Hanrahan: 'Trice, didn't you tell me that he was supposed to die in his sleep?
>
> Seibert: If that would happen, 'cause he was on that new medicine, you know ... .
>
> Hanrahan: The Prozac? And it makes him sleepy. So he was supposed to die in his sleep?
>
> Seibert: Yes.

Based largely on her confession to Hanrahan, Seibert was charged with first-degree murder for her role in Rector's death. Seibert asked to have all of her statements, both before and after the *Miranda* warnings, suppressed.

At the suppression hearing, Hanrahan testified that he had deliberately withheld *Miranda* warnings as part of a well-known interrogation technique, "question first," which he had learned in police training courses.

First, you ask the questions meant to get the suspect to confess, he explained. You know that any incriminating statements the suspect makes at this stage will not be permitted in court.

PATRICE SEIBERT WAS CONVICTED OF THE MURDER OF HER TWELVE-YEAR-OLD SON, LARGELY ON THE BASIS OF A CONFESSION SHE MADE BEFORE SHE WAS READ HER *MIRANDA* RIGHTS. HER CONVICTION WAS OVERTURNED BY THE SUPREME COURT IN 2004 BECAUSE IT HAD BEEN COERCED.

Then, after giving the suspect a short break, you read her the *Miranda* warnings. Typically, the suspect will waive her right to a lawyer since she had already confessed, as Seibert had.

Then you repeat those same questions until the suspect gives you back the same answers she gave you the first time, before you placed her under arrest. Hanrahan admitted that Seibert's confession was largely a repeat of information she had given him before he'd read her the warnings.

Seibert's statements before the *Miranda* warnings were suppressed, but the statements she made afterward

GOOD COP, BAD COP

Law officers have a battery of strategies to choose from when interrogating a suspect. One that you may have seen on television cop shows is known as "good cop, bad cop." It's a legal interrogation strategy, and it works like this.

Two officers work as partners. One takes the role of Good Cop. He or she acts friendly and courteous toward the suspect, while the partner, Bad Cop, acts hostile and menacing. They take turns asking the suspect questions and responding to his answers.

Good Cop responds with sympathy even when the suspect is not cooperating, while Bad Cop responds with mounting impatience and anger. If the suspect still refuses to confess, Bad Cop blows his stack and gets violent. He may strike the table or wall with his fists or toss a chair.

Finally, as Bad Cop threatens to turn his violent behavior on the suspect, Good Cop grabs his partner and shoves him out of the room. It's all an act, but it often works. Alone now with Good Cop, the relieved but shook-up and frightened suspect is ready to confess.

were allowed as evidence, and Seibert was convicted
of second-degree murder.

MISSOURI V. SEIBERT (2004)

Seibert won her appeal to the Missouri Supreme State
Court. The court ruled that Seibert's second set of incriminating statements were clearly the product of the illegally
obtained first set, and so should be suppressed.

The state of Missouri then appealed that ruling to the
U.S. Supreme Court, which accepted the appeal because
it presented a new challenge to *Miranda*. The question
facing the Court was this: Should the answers from a
second phase of questioning after *Miranda* warnings,
like the one Patrice Seibert went through, be used in
trial court?

The decision would hinge on the question-first
technique. To testify about it, the Court called on an
expert witness:

> An officer of [the Rolla, Missouri] police depart-
> ment testified that the strategy of withholding
> *Miranda* warnings until after interrogating and
> drawing out a confession was promoted not only
> by his own department, but by a national police
> training organization and other departments in
> which he had worked.

Papers filed with the Court confirmed that the
question-first technique was used by police in thirty-
eight different states. In its ruling, the Court described
the goal of the technique this way:

> The object of question-first is to render *Miranda*
> warnings ineffective by waiting for a particularly

opportune time to give them, after the suspect has already confessed.

What psychological effect might this technique have on a suspect? The Court stated: "[T]elling a suspect that 'anything you say can and will be used against you,' without expressly excepting the statement just given, could lead to an entirely reasonable inference that what he has just said will be used, with subsequent silence being of no avail."

When the *Miranda* warnings were inserted in the midst of an interrogation, the Court said, they were likely to mislead and "deprive a defendant of knowledge essential to his ability to understand the nature of his rights and the consequences of abandoning them."

That is, the question-first technique turns the *Miranda* warnings around and makes them a weapon for the police to use to coerce the suspect into confessing. For all these reasons, the Court ruled in favor of Seibert and against the question-first technique.

Evaluating *Miranda*

The *Seibert* ruling can be looked at in two very different ways. You could see it as a refinement of *Miranda* that leads to guilty people going free. Or you could see it as a ruling that effectively protects suspects from police coercion.

One legal expert, lawyer Edward Lazarus, calls both these viewpoints extreme and untrue. *Miranda* "is neither unloosing thousands of criminals onto our streets," he writes, "nor protecting criminal defendants against the worst of police misconduct." Instead, "[O]ur legal system has accommodated itself to *Miranda*, so as to make of the doctrine a surprisingly useful compromise between those extremes."

Statistics about suppressed confessions continue to show that *Miranda* is not turning thousands of criminals back onto the street. U.S. Justice Department records show that between 1989 and 1999, *Miranda* violations led to federal courts suppressing only about 2 out of every 9,300 confessions. On the other hand, accusations of police brutality continue to be made by suspects across the nation.

But *Miranda* clearly has helped protect the rights of criminal suspects. And in protecting their rights, it probably has made law enforcement more difficult, at least in some instances. But is that necessarily a bad thing?

Justice Hugo Black, who was on the majority side in *Miranda*, addressed this question publicly in 1968. He was the subject of an hour-long TV interview with CBS newsman Martin Agronsky, called "Justice Black and the Bill of Rights." In this exchange from the interview, the two are speaking of *Miranda* and other U.S. Supreme Court decisions, such as *Malloy* and *Escobedo*, that broaden and strengthen a suspect's rights.

> Agronsky: Mr. Justice, do you think that those decisions have made it more difficult for the police to combat crime?
>
> Black: Certainly. Why shouldn't they? What were they written for? Why did they write the Bill of Rights? They practically all relate to the way cases should be tried. And practically all of them make it more difficult to convict people of crime. What about guaranteeing a man a right to a lawyer? Of course that makes it more diffi-

cult to convict him. What about saying he shall not be compelled to be a witness against himself? That makes it more difficult to convict him. . . . They were, every one, intended to make it more difficult before the doors of a prison closed on a man because of his trial.

ErneSTO MIranDa HIMSeLF

We have seen what has become of the *Miranda* ruling since the Court's 1966 decision. We have learned how it has become an accepted and effective part of police work today, yet subject to constant challenge and refinement in the courts.

But what of the man himself? What about Ernesto Miranda? First, we need to remember that a U.S. Supreme Court decision that reverses a conviction based on *Miranda* violations does not free the suspect. Instead, the case is sent back to the state courts, where often the suspect is tried again and found guilty even without the confession that now must be suppressed.

A confession usually signals to police that a crime has been solved, and so they stop investigating the crime and turn their attention to other cases. This may mean that there is still evidence waiting to be uncovered that may become part of the retrial and lead to a conviction.

The state of Arizona re-tried Miranda in 1967, and the outcome rested largely on a new piece of evidence. In this instance it came from the suspect himself. Miranda sealed his own fate on March 16, 1963, when his common-law wife, Twila Hoffman, and one of her daughters—not the one Miranda had fathered—paid him a visit. At the time Miranda was in jail awaiting his first trial on robbery and rape.

At the retrial, four years later and after the U.S. Supreme Court ruling, Hoffman testified that she left the jail that day in 1963 in a state of fear. Miranda had admitted to her that he was guilty of the rape. Hoffman also testified that she had good reason to believe that if Ernesto Miranda were ever to get out of prison, he would try to harm her daughter.

Hoffman's testimony at the retrial helped convict Miranda for a second time and send him back to the Arizona State Prison at Florence. While in prison, Miranda made himself useful. He learned to cut hair and became the warden's personal barber. He also behaved himself, and as a result, was let out on parole in December 1971.

Miranda emerged from prison an infamous man. A lot of people knew who he was, but they also knew about the violent acts he'd committed. Miranda thought it would be a good idea to cash in on his infamy. So he had cards printed up that were similar to the *Miranda* rights cards police all over the nation now carried. For $1.50 you could buy a card and have it autographed by Ernesto Miranda personally, on the steps of the Maricopa County Courthouse in Phoenix.

Miranda managed to stay out of jail until August 1974, when he was picked up on charges of possession of guns and narcotics. Since these were violations of his parole, he was sent back to prison in January 1975.

A year later he was out again and delivering appliances for a store in Phoenix. But he was also finding ways to get himself into trouble. Miranda was playing poker one night with two illegal Mexican immigrants at a Phoenix bar when the three men got into an argument that turned into a fistfight that turned into a murder. Miranda was stabbed to death.

The killer was arrested shortly afterwards. Ironically, the first thing the policeman did while arresting Ernesto Miranda's killer was read him his *Miranda* rights.

NOTES

Chapter One
p.11, par. 2, "Ernesto *Miranda.*" WorldHistory.com.
www.worldhistory.com/wiki/E/Ernesto-*Miranda*.htm
p.16, par. 2, *Miranda* v. *Arizona*, 384 U.S. 436 (1966). Findlaw.com
laws.findlaw.com/us/384/436.html
p.16, par. 3, Ibid.

Chapter Two
p.18, par. 2, *Miranda*, Ibid.
p.21, par. 1, *Miranda*, Ibid.
p.22, par. 1, "The Courts." Shakespeare Law Library.
www.sourcetext.com/lawlibrary/underhill/o1.htm.
p.23, par. 3, *Brown et al.* v. *State of Mississippi* (1936). The Injustice Line.
www.injusticeline.com/brown.html
p.24, par. 1, *Miranda*, Ibid.
p.26, par. 1, Quoted in *Miranda*, Ibid.
p.26, par. 4, Quoted in *Miranda*, Ibid.
p.26, par. 5, *Miranda*, Ibid. Quoted in *Miranda*, Ibid.
p.28, par. 1, *Miranda*, Ibid. Quoted in *Miranda*, Ibid.
p.28, par. 1, Quoted in *Miranda*, Ibid.
p.30, par. 1, *Brown*, Ibid.

Chapter Three
p.35, par. 1, Douglas Linder. "The Trial of the Scottsboro Boys." *Jurist*.
www.jurist.law.pitt.edu/trials4.htm
p.37, par. 6–p.38, par. 1, *Powell* v. *State of Alabama*, 287 U.S. 45 (1932).
Findlaw.com.caselaw.lp.findlaw.com/scripts/getcase.pl?court=US&v
ol=287&invol=45
p.38, par. 2, *Powell*, Ibid.
p.39, par. 4, *Powell*, Ibid.
p.39, par. 5, *Betts* v. *Brady*, 316 U.S. 455 (1942). Findlaw.com.

caselaw.lp.findlaw.com/cgibin/getcase.PL?court=US&vol=316
&invol=455

p.39, par. 6–p.40, par. 1, *Betts*, Ibid.

p.40, par. 4, *Betts*, Ibid.

p.40, par. 5, *Betts*, Ibid.

p.42, par. 4–p.43, par. 1, *Gideon* v. *Wainwright*, 372 U.S. 335 (1963).
Findlaw.com.caselaw.lp.findlaw.com/scripts/getcase.pl?court=us&v
ol=372&invol=335

p.43, par. 2, Ibid.

p.44, par. 1, Quoted in *Gideon*, Ibid.

p.45, par. 1, *Gideon*, Ibid.

p.45, par. 2, Quoted in *Gideon*, Ibid.

p.45, par. 4, *Gideon*, Ibid.

p.46, par. 1, *Gideon*, Ibid.

p.46, par. 3, Liva Baker. *Miranda: Crime, Law and Politics*. New York:
Atheneum, 1983, p. 82.

p.48, par. 1, *Escobedo* v. *Illinois*, 378 U.S. 478 (1964). Findlaw.com.
laws.findlaw.com/us/378/478.html

p.48, par. 2, *Escobedo*, Ibid.

p.48, par. 4, *Escobedo*, Ibid.

p.48, par. 5, *Escobedo*, Ibid.

p.49, par. 1, *Escobedo*, Ibid.

p.50, par. 2, *Miranda*, Ibid.

p.50, par. 4, *Escobedo*, Ibid.

p.51, par. 1, Baker, 158.

p.51, par. 2, Baker, 161.

Chapter Four

p.56, par. 1, "Rules of the Supreme Court of the United States."
January 27, 2003. www.supremecourtus.gov/ctrules/rulesofthe
court.pdf

p.56, par. 4, Baker, p. 63.

p.56, par. 5, "Rules," Ibid.

p.57, par. 3, Baker, p. 83.

p.58, par. 1, Baker, p. 103.

p.58, par. 4, Baker, p. 105.

p.59, par. 5–p.60, par. 1, *Miranda*, Ibid.

p.61, par. 2, *Miranda* v. *Arizona*, Brief for Petitioner. United States
Supreme Court Records and Briefs. curiae.law.yale.edu/pdf/384-
436/008.pdf

p.61, par. 2, "Ernesto *Miranda*," Ibid.

p.62, par. 4, *Miranda* v. *Arizona*, ACLU Brief. United States Supreme
Court Records and Briefs. curiae.law.yale.edu/pdf/384-436/017.pdf,
pp. 59 and 63.

p.63, par. 1, Baker, p. 108.

Chapter Five

p.64, par. 4–p.65, par. 1, "How the Court Works." The Supreme Court Historical Society.

www.supremecourthistory.org/03_how/subs_how/03_a07.html

p.65, par. 3, *Miranda* v. *Arizona*, Brief for Petitioner, Ibid.

p.65, par. 4, Ibid.

p.65, par. 5, Ibid.

p.65, par. 6–p.66, par. 1, Ibid.

p.66, par. 2, *Escobedo*, Ibid.

p.66, par. 3, *Miranda* v. *Arizona*, Brief for Petitioner, Ibid.

p.66, par. 5, Quoted in *Miranda* v. *Arizona*, Brief for Petitioner, Ibid.

p.67, par. 1, *Miranda* v. *Arizona*, Brief for Petitioner, Ibid.

p.67, par. 2, Ibid.

p.67, par. 3, Ibid.

p.68, par. 3, *Miranda* v. *Arizona*, Respondent's Brief. United States Supreme Court Records and Briefs. curiae.law.yale.edu/pdf/ 384-436/013.pdf

p.68, par. 6–p.69, par. 1, Ibid.

p.69, par. 3, Ibid.

p.69, par. 4, Ibid.

p.69, par. 6–p.70, par. 1, Ibid.

p.70, par. 2, Ibid.

p.70, par. 4, Ibid.

p.71, par. 6, Dahlia Lithwick. "Specter Resurrected." *Slate Magazine*, November 19, 2004. slate.msn.com/id/2109983.

p.72, par. 2, *Minnesota* v. *Carter*, (1998). Findlaw.com. caselaw.lp.findlaw.com/scripts/getcase.pl?court=US&vol=000 &invol=97-1147

p.74, par. 7–p.75, par. 1, Gideon v. Wainwright, Oral Argument. www.oyez.org/oyez/resource/case/139/audioresources.

Chapter Six

p.78, par. 2, *Miranda* v. *Arizona*, Ibid.

p.79, par. 1, Ibid.

p.79, par. 2, Ibid.

p.79, par. 4, Ibid.

p.80, par. 1, Ibid.

p.80, par. 2, Ibid.

p.80, par. 3, Ibid.

p.81, par. 2, Ibid.

p.81, par. 3, Ibid.

p.81, par. 5, Ibid.

p.82, par. 2, Ibid.

p.82, par. 4, Ibid.

p.82, par. 6, Ibid.

p.84, par. 5–p.85, par. 1, Ibid.

p.85, par. 2, Ibid.

p.85, par. 3, Ibid.

p.85, par. 5–p.86, par. 1, Ibid.

p.86, par. 3, Ibid.

p.86, par. 5–p.87, par. 1, Ibid.

p.87, par. 3, Ibid.

p.87, par. 5, Ibid.

p.88, par. 2, Baker, p. 66.

p.89, par. 2, Michael C. Dorf. "How Reliable Is Eyewitness Testimony?" *FindLaw's Legal Commentary*. May 16, 2000. writ.news.findlaw.com/dorf/20010516.html

Chapter Seven

p.91, par. 1, Baker, 66. *Miranda* v. *Arizona*, ibid.

p.92, par. 2, "*Miranda* Law: A Guide to the Privilege Against Self-Incrimination." faculty.ncwc.edu/toconnor/miranda.htm.

p.93, par. 1, Baker, p. 40.

p.93, par. 2, "U.S. Homicide Rate (per 100,000)." Crime in the United States, 2002, FBI, Uniform Crime Reports. www.infoplease.com/ipa/A0873729.html

p.94, par. 2, Baker, p. 211.

p.94, par. 4, *Miranda* v. *Arizona*, Ibid.

p.95, par. 1, "Statutory Law 3501." University of Utah, S. J. Quinney College of Law. www.law.utah.edu/faculty/websites/cassellp/*Miranda*/text3501. html

p.95, par. 5, Gail Blasser Riley. Miranda *v.* Arizona: *Rights of the Accused*. Hillside, New Jersey: Enslow, 1994, p. 99.

p.96, par. 1, Riley, Ibid, p. 100.

p.96, par. 1, Riley, Ibid, p. 99.

p.96, par. 2, Peter Baird. "Fighting Crime by the Rules." *Newsweek*, July 18, 1988, p. 53.

p.96, par. 4, *New York* v. *Quarles*, 467 U.S. 648 (1984). Findlaw.com. caselaw.lp.findlaw.com/scripts/getcase.pl?court=us &vol=467&invol=649

Chapter Eight

p.97, par. 2, *Dickerson* v. *United States* 530 U.S. 428 (2000). Findlaw.com. caselaw.lp.findlaw.com/scripts/getcase.pl?court=us &vol=000&invol=99-5525

p.100, par. 4, *New York* v. *Quarles*, Ibid.

p.101, par. 2, *Illinois* v. *Perkins*, 496 U.S. 292 (1990). Findlaw.com. caselaw.lp.findlaw.com/scripts/getcase.pl?court=US &vol=496&invol=292

p.101, par. 6–p.102, par. 1, Ibid.

p.102, par. 2, Ibid.

p.103, par. 2, *Argersinger* v. *Hamlin*, 407 U.S. 25 (1972). Findlaw.com. caselaw.lp.findlaw.com/scripts/getcase.pl?navby= case&court=us&vol=407&page=35

p.104, par. 1, *Edwards* v. *Arizona*, 451 U.S. 477 (1981). Findlaw.com. caselaw.lp.findlaw.com/scripts/printer_friendly.pl?page=us/451/ 477.html

p.104, par. 5, *Minnick* v. *Mississippi*, 498 U.S. 146 (1990). Findlaw.com. caselaw.lp.findlaw.com/scripts/printer_friendly.pl? page=us/498/146.html

p.105, par. 2, Ibid.

Chapter Nine

p.108, par. 3, *Dickerson* v. *United States*, Ibid.

p.108, par. 4, Terry Frieden. "Government Files Brief Seeking to Preserve *Miranda* Warnings." November 2, 1999. CNN.com www.cnn.com/us/9911/02/Miranda.warnings.01/index.html

p.109, par. 2–p.110, par. 1, "*Miranda* Law," Ibid.

p.110, par. 5, "Brief of Federal Bureau of Investigation Agents Association as *amicus curiae* in support of the United States Court of Appeals for the Fourth Circuit." University of Utah, S.J. Quinney College of Law. www.law.utah.edu/faculty/websites/ cassellp/fbibrief.html

p.111, par. 1, *Dickerson* v. *United States*, Ibid.

p.111, par. 2, Ibid.

p.111, par. 3, Ibid.

p.111, par. 4, Ibid.

p.111, par. 5, Terry Frieden, Ibid.

p.112, par. 2, *Dickerson* v. *United States*, Ibid.

p.112, par. 4, Ibid.

p.112, par. 5, Ibid.

Chapter Ten

p.113, par. 1, "*Miranda* Rights Reread." *The Nation*. July 17, 2000. www.thenation.com/doc.mhtml?i=20000717&s=editors

p.113, par. 3, Richard Willing. "High Court to Debate *Miranda* Rights, Again." USA Today. December 7, 2003. www.usatoday.com/news/washington/2003-12-07-Miranda- usat_x.htm

p.116, par. 3, *Yarborough* v. *Alvarado* (02-1684) 316 F .3d 841. Findlaw.com. caselaw.lp.findlaw.com/scripts/getcase.pl?court=US &vol=496&involv=292

p.116, par. 5, Ibid.

p.116, par. 6–p.117, par. 1, Ibid.

p.118, par. 8–p.119, par. 1, *Fellers* v. *United States* (02-6320). Findlaw.com. caselaw.lp.findlaw.com/scripts/getcase.pl?court=US &vol=000&invol=02-6320

p.120, par. 3, *Missouri* v. *Seibert* (02-1371). Findlaw.com. caselaw.lp.findlaw.com/scripts/getcase.pl?court=US&vol=000 &invol=02-1371

p.123, par. 5, Ibid.

p.123, par. 6, Richard Willing, Ibid.

p.123, par. 7–p.124, par. 1, *Missouri* v. *Seibert*, Ibid.

p.124, par. 2, Ibid.

p.124, par. 3, Ibid.

p.124, par. 6–p.125, par. 1, Edward Lazarus. "How *Miranda* Really Works and Why It Really Matters." CNN.com. June 7, 2000. www.cnn.com/2000/LAW/06/columns/lazarus.06.07/

p.125, par. 2, Paul Cassell. "Time to Overhaul *Miranda*?" University of Utah, S. J. Quinney College of Law. www.law.utah.edu/faculty/websites/cassellp/main5.html

p.125, par. 5–p.126, par. 1, Elizabeth Black. "Hugo Black: A Memorial Portrait." The Supreme Court Historical Society, 1982 Yearbook. www.supremecourthistory.org/04_library/subs_volumes/04_c17_j.html

(All Internet sites were accessible as of February 15, 2005.)

FurTHer InformaTion

FURTHER READING
Haskins, James. *The Scottsboro Boys*. New York: Holt, 1993.

Herda, D. J. *Earl Warren: Chief Justice for Social Change*. Springfield,
New Jersey: Enslow Publishers, 1995.

Kowalski, Kathiann M. *Order in the Court: A Look at the Judicial
Branch*. Minneapolis, MN: Lerner Publications, 2004.

Lewis, Anthony. *Gideon's Trumpet*. New York: Random House, 1964.

McKissack, Pat. *To Establish Justice: Citizenship and the Constitution*.
New York: Knopf, 2004.

Meltzer, Milton. *The Right to Remain Silent*. New York: Harcourt
Brace Jovanovich, 1972.

Morin, Isobel V. *Our Changing Constitution: How and Why We Have
Amended It*. Brookfield, CT: Millbrook Press, 1998.

The Oxford Companion to the Supreme Court of the United States.
New York: Oxford University Press, 1992.

WEB SITES
These Web sites are good places to pick up information and ideas on
the issues discussed in this book.

Findlaw.com
www.findlaw.com/casecode/supreme.html
Free, easy-to-search database of U.S. Supreme Court opinions
dating back to 1893.

The 'Lectric Law Library *Lawcopedia's* Constitutional Law & Rights
Topic Area
www.lectlaw.com/tcon.htm
Information on a wide variety of legal issues connected with constitutional rights.

Miranda Rights and Related Cases
www.thecapras.org/mcapra/miranda/rights.html
A site that offers a large collection of legal documents and news sto-
ries related to *Miranda* v. *Arizona*.

The U.S. Constitution Online
www.usconstitution.net
This site, aimed at young people, gives an in-depth look at the
Constitution, the Bill of Rights, the Declaration of Independence,
and some state constitutions. Includes frequently asked questions,
a timeline, and a section on the Miranda warning.

United States Supreme Court
www.supremecourtus.gov
Official site of the nation's highest court, packed with information on
the history of the Court, how the Court works, and its current cases.

BIBLIOGraPHY

BOOKS

Baker, Liva. *Miranda: Crime, Law, and Politics*. New York: Atheneum, 1983.

Riley, Gail Blasser. Miranda *v.* Arizona: *Rights of the Accused*. Hillside, NJ: Enslow Publishers, 1994.

MIRANDA BRIEFS

ACLU: curiae.law.yale.edu/pdf/384-436/017.pdf

National District Attorneys Association: curiae.law.yale.edu/pdf/384-436/012.pdf

Respondent: curiae.law.yale.edu/pdf/384-436/013.pdf

Petitioner: curiae.law.yale.edu/pdf/384-436/008.pdf

FBIAA:www.law.utah.edu/faculty/websites/cassellp/fbibrief.html

MIRANDA RULING

laws.findlaw.com/us/384/436.html

RELATED CASES

Argersinger v. *Hamlin*, 407 U.S. 25 (1972).

Betts v. *Brady*, 316 U.S. 455 (1942).

Brown et al. v. *State of Mississippi* (1936).

Dickerson v. *United States* 530 U.S. 428 (2000).

Edwards v. *Arizona*, 451 U.S. 477 (1981).

Escobedo v. *Illinois*, 378 U.S. 478 (1964).

Fellers v. *United States* (02-6320).

Gideon v. *Wainwright*, 372 U.S. 335 (1963).

Illinois v. *Perkins*, 496 U.S. 292 (1990).

Minnick v. *Mississippi*, 498 U.S. 146 (1990).

Missouri v. *Seibert* (02-1371).

New York v. *Quarles*, 467 U.S. 648 (1984).

Powell v. *State of Alabama*, 287 U.S. 45 (1932).

Yarborough v. *Alvarado* (02-1684) 316 F .3d 841.

INDEX

Page numbers in **boldface** are illustrations, tables, and charts

activist stance, 41, **42**, **54**, 72–74, 77, 99, 111

African Americans, 26, 28, 34, **36**

Agronsky, Martin, 125

Alvarado, Michael, 114–117

American Civil Liberties Union (ACLU), 56, 61–63

amicus curiae briefs, 61–63, 110

appellate courts, purpose of, 13–14

Argersinger v. *Hamlin*, 102, 103

Bates, Ruby, 38

Bell, Griffin, 96

Betts v. *Brady*, 33, 39–41, 42, 43, 65

Bill of Rights, 21, 28, 41, 125

Black, Hugo L., 40, 43–45, **44**, 53, **73**, 74, 77, 125–126

Blackmun, Harry A., 99

Brennan, William J. Jr., **73**, 74, 77

briefs, 60–63, 65–71, 108, 110–111

Brown, Ed, 28

Brown v. *Board of Education*, 41

Brown v. *Mississippi*, 18, 23, 28, 30, 34, 38, 52, 78, 105

Brown v. *Walker*, 18, 26

Burger, Warren, 99

California v. *Stewart*, 58, 59, 60, 79

capital cases, 25, 34, 39, 40, 42, 49–50, 65, 104

Cassell, Paul, 109, **109**

certiorari, writ of (cert), 55, 57–58, 60, 98

Charlton, Donald, 100

Clark, Tom C., **73**, 74, 77, **90**, 91, 95

compelling reason for review, 55–56

confession, 49, 58–63, 66, 97, 100, 112, 113, 114, 117–119

coerced, 10–14, 16, 19, **19**, 21,
   23–24, 26, 28, 30, 51–53
danger of coercion, 79, 82, **83**,
   85–87, 96, 110, 116, 119–121,
   121, 124
discouraging, 87, 90–91, 95
false, 28, 29, **83**
new voluntary standards, 82, 84
suppressed, 78, 96, 98–99, 104,
   107, 118, 125–126
voluntary, 21, 24, 28, 51–53, 63,
   68–70, 79–80, 85, 94–96, 103,
   105, 108, 110–111
Cooley, Carroll, 9, 12, 14
counsel, right to, 16, 33–53, 57–
   61, 63, 65, 92, 98, 119–121
extension of, 102–103
as growing right, 65–68, 71–72,
   78, 80–82, **83**, 84–85, 89, 104,
   112, 125
Court of the Star Chamber, 19, **19**,
   21–23, **22**, **23**, 29, 67, 73
crier, 64
criminals, rights of, 10, **23**, 33,
   42, 50, **51**, 66
advocates for, 53
Miranda and, 14, 18, 74, 94, 125
custody factor, 114–117, 118

Department of Justice (DOJ), 108,
   111, 125
Dickerson, Charles, 107–108, 110,
   113
Dickerson v. *United States*, 107–113,
   109

DiGerlando, Benedict, 47–48, 49
dissenting opinion, 40, 50, **51**, 72,
   105, **106**, 112
   Miranda, 86–87, 89, **90**, 91
Douglas, William O., 53, 66, **73**,
   74, 77
due process, 25, 30, 31, 38–41, 52

Edwards v. *Arizona*, 103–104
Ellington, Arthur, 28
English common law, 21
Escobedo, Daniel, 47, **47**, 48–49,
   52, 68
Escobedo v. *Illinois*, 33, 41–42,
   46–52, **51**, 57
   Miranda and, 58–61, 66–68, 78,
   98, 125
evidence, 13, 24, 44, 111
   confessions as, 49–51, 59–60, 69,
   80, 84–85, 89, 101, 105, 107–108,
   123
   suppression of, 10–12, 16, 60–
   61, 70, 84, 96, 101, 108, 111, 118,
   121, 123, 125
exclusionary rule, 10
eyewitness, 87, 88, 89

Federal Bureau of Investigation
   (FBI), 58, 79, 93, 95
Federal Bureau of Investigation
   Agents Association (FBIAA), 110
Fellers, John, 118, 119
Fellers v. *United States*, 118–119
felony case, 7, 8, 49, 50, 102
Flynn, John J., 56, 57, 60, 66

Fortas, Abe, **73**, 74–75, **75**, 78, 99
Frank, John, 51, 56, 57, 60, 66, 89

Gideon, Clarence Earl, 42–45, **43**
Gideon v. Wainwright, 33, 41–46,
   43, **44**, 49, 65–66, 74, 78, 102
Goldwater, Barry, 93
good cop, bad cop, 122

habeas corpus, writ of, 47
Hanrahan, Richard, 119, 120–121
Harlan, John M., **73**, 74, 86–87
Harris, Vivien, 98, 99
Harris v. New York, 98–99
Hoffman, Twila, 8, 126–127

Illinois v. Perkins, 100–102
impeaching witnesses, 98–99
impeachment, 41–42, **42**, 98
interrogation, 9, 16, 26, 29, 47–50,
   47, 52, **83**, 119
   legal definition, 117
   Miranda and, 57–60, 66–70, 72,
     75, 78–82, 84–85, 89, 96,
     101–102, 107
   strategies, 62–63, 79, 85, 118,
     121, 122, 123–124
   warning before, **90**, 91, 110–112,
     114, 118

"jolting" technique, 62

Lazarus, Edward, 124
Lilburn, John, **20**, 21, 73

Lilburn Star Chamber case, 18,
   21, 24

majority opinion, 40, 41, 43–45,
   44, 50, 111
Miranda, **76**, 77–82, 84–86, 91,
   112
Malloy, William, 30
Malloy v. Hogan, 18, 30, 32, 78,
   125
Marshall, Thurgood, 96
Merola, Mario, 96
Minnick v. Mississippi, 104–105,
   112
minors, 8, 29, 114, 115, 116
Miranda, Ernesto, **6**, 7–9, 33, 51,
   56, 67, 126–128
   the appeals process, 13–14
   confession, 9–11, 81
   crimes, 8–9
   jury trial, 12–13
   pre-trial hearing, 11–12
   Supreme Court ruling, 14, **75**, 78
Miranda cards, 92, **92**, 127
Miranda ruling, 7–9, 16–18, 24,
   28, **76**, 77–89, 112–113, 124–126
   exceptions, 97–102, 110, 113
   extensions, 97, 102–104, **106**,
     113
   limits to rights, 82, 84, 85
   new challenges to, 114–124
   reaction to, 93–96, 108
   rights explained, 80–82, **83**, 84
Miranda v. Arizona, 14, 16, 18, 21,
   40, 53

briefs, 60, 61–63
challenges to, 107–111, **109**
decision, 71, **73**, 74–75, **75**, **76**,
   77–89, 112
decisions influencing, 18, 33, 50
filing the case, 55–63
oral argument, 60–61, 64–71,
   78
Miranda warning, 84, 92, 94–96,
   99–101, 103, 107–108, 110,
   114–115, 117, 120–121, **121**,
   123–124, 128
misdemeanor, defined, 102, 103
Missouri v. *Seibert*, 123–124
Moody, Milo, 37, 38
Moore, Alvin, 11–12, 56

National District Attorneys
   Association, 63
Nelson, Gary K., 61, 67–71, 81
New York v. *Quarles*, 99
"not guilty" plea, 24, 25, 45

Omnibus Crime Control and Safe
   Streets Act of 1968, 94

Patterson, Aaron, **83**
Perkins, Lloyd, 100–101
petitioner, defined, 14
police abuse, 14, 24, 109, 124
   brutality, 26, 28, 53, 58, 70,
      83, 86
   interrogation techniques, 62–63,
      79, 85, 118, 121–124

police lineup, 9, 88, **88**
Powell, Ozie, 37
Powell v. *Alabama*, 33, 34, 37–39,
   44–45, 60, 65, 67, 102, 105
precedent, defined, 18, 43, 79
pre–trial hearing, defined, 11–12
pro bono tradition, 56
prohibition, 27
Prynne, William, 23
public safety, concern for, 99,
   100

Quarles, Benjamin, 99
question-first technique, 119–124

rack torture, **22**, 23, 30
Rector, Donald, 119–120, 121
respondent, defined, 14
Roddy, Stephen, 37, 38

Scalia, Antonin, 72, 105, **106**, 112
Scottsboro boys, 34–38, **35**, **36**
Seibert, Patrice, 119–124, **121**
self-incrimination, 21, 24–25, 30,
   60, 63, 79–82, 86–87, 94, 112,
   119–123, 126
Shields, Henry, 28
silence, right to, 18–32, 49, 57–59,
   68, 71, 81, 92, 94
   extension to, 103–104, 105
Simpson, Cuthbert, **22**
statutory law 3501, 94, 95, 107–111
Stewart, Potter, 73, 74, 77, 86
Stewart, Roy Allen, 59

"strategic interruptions," 62
strict constructionists, 72, 73,
   77, 87, 99, 111, 112

"the third degree," 26, 28
torture, 22–23, **22**, **23**, 29, 30
totality-of-circumstances standard, 52, 53, 84, 95, 108, 111
Townsend, Jerry Frank, 29

the undercover agent, 100–102
U.S. Constitution, 15, 56, 87
   Eighteenth Amendment, 27
   Fifth Amendment, 18, 21, 25, 28,
      30–32, 56–57, 59, 67, 71–72,
      78, 80, 85, 87, 113
   Fourteenth Amendment, 30,
      31, 41, 65
   Sixth Amendment, 33–34, 40,
      43, 56–59, 65–68, 71–72, 78,
      98, 103,118–119
U.S. criminal justice system, 10,
   24, 50, 110
appellate courts, 13–14
U.S. homicide rate, 93
U.S. Supreme Court, 15, 28, 30,
   34, 38, 64–65
   Miranda ruling, 14–18, 71–73,
      76, 77–89
   and state courts, 28, 30, 34, 38

victims, rights of, 10, 69, 94
Vignera, Michael, 58
Vignera v. *New York*, 58

violent crime, 69–70, 87, 93, 127

Warren, Earl, 41–42, **42**, **54**, **73**,
   74, 75, 99
   Miranda ruling, 76, 77–79
Warren Court, 41–42, 73–74, 111
Westover, Carl Calvin, 58, 59
Westover v. *United States*, 58–59,
   79
White, Byron R., 50, 51, **51**, **73**,
   74, 77, 86
Wickersham Commission, 26
Wickersham Report, 26, 28, 117
Wilson, Orlando, 51
Wolfson, Warren, 48
Wright, Roy, 37

Yarborough v. *Alvarado*, 114–117
Young, Wilfred, 9, 12, 14

aBOUT THE auTHOr

RON FrIDeLL has written for radio, television, news-papers, and textbooks. He has written books on social and political issues, such as terrorism and espionage, and scientific topics, such as DNA fingerprinting and global warming. His most recent book for Marshall Cavendish Benchmark is *Environmental Issues* in our Open for Debate series. He taught English as a second language while a member of the Peace Corp in Bangkok, Thailand. He lives in Evanston, Illinois, with his wife Patricia and his dog, an Australian Shepherd named Madeline.